Contents

6 Advanced Excel functions 95

8 Advanced PowerPoint functions 133

Introduction

This book will help you to become acquainted with Office XP and to discover all the new features that have been introduced. Whether you are a beginner or an expert user, this book is meant for you, because it explains all the procedures proposed by Microsoft for you to be able to work quickly and easily. It also suggests expert tips and tricks to improve your performance.

How do I use this book?

Since the chapters are independent of each other, you can read them in the order you choose. To find a command quickly, consult the index at the end of the book. The book is structured as follows:

- Chapters 1 and 2 are a quick introduction to Office XP. You will discover the various interface features as well as the commands which are shared by all the applications: opening a file, saving, and so on.
- Chapters 3 and 4 teach you how to use basic and more advanced Word functions.
- Chapters 5 and 6 explain how to use Excel.
- Chapters 7 and 8 are dedicated to creating presentations with PowerPoint.
- Chapters 9 and 10 deal with Outlook.

Adopted conventions

All commands are displayed in bold. Throughout the text, a number of symbols alert you to terminology issues and technical details, and indicate shortcuts or advice to the user:

 Gives you additional information.

 Warns you about problems you may encounter in certain cases. If you follow the instructions, you should not have any problems.

 Provides you with suggestions and tips, including keyboard shortcuts, advanced techniques, and so on.

 This icon indicates features new to Office XP.

Help, checks and Web tools

Office Assistant

Help

Wizards and templates

Spelling and grammar

Find and Replace

Office XP and the Web

The functions you are going to discover in this chapter are shared—by all Office applications.

*If the Office Assistant does not come up when you launch the application click on the **Help** button in the Standard toolbar in the active application.*

In this chapter, we will look at the various procedures you can follow to get help. We will also look at the tools you need to speed up your work, check spelling and grammar, and so on.

Office Assistant

Introduced with Office 97, the Office Assistant takes you through all operations. If you are not familiar with version 97, the Office Assistant is a little paper clip that works very hard to provide advice when you need it. A faithful, effective and competent assistant, it never fails you.

When you launch an Office application, the Office Assistant is activated by default (Figure 1.1).

To ask the Office Assistant a question, click on it. Type the question in the text area (Figure 1.2), then click on **Search**. A list of icons is displayed; click on the one that corresponds to your search. If the list of icons is not relevant, click on **Next** to display the follow-up.

To hide the Office Assistant, click on **?** in the Menu bar, then select **Hide Office Assistant**.

Office Assistant options

You can modify the Office Assistant default options. For example, you can choose a different look:

1. Click with the right mouse button (right-click) on the assistant, then select **Choose Assistant**.

Figure 1.1 As soon as you start an application, the Office Assistant is displayed.

Figure 1.2 Ask the Office Assistant a question.

*If you prefer, you can turn off the Assistant and get help through the **Ask a question** box in the top right of the application window.*

For some tasks, the Office Assistant may offer help of its own accord. In this case it displays a text balloon. Click on the assistant to view its advice.

Figure 1.3 The Options tab in the Office Assistant dialog box allows you to set options for this function.

2. Click on the **Gallery** tab. Scroll through the various types of assistants by clicking on the **Next** button or the **Back** button. The display area shows the 'face' of the selected assistant.

3. Once you have specified your choice, click on **OK** to confirm.

To modify the Office Assistant options, click on the **Options** tab in the Office Assistant dialog box (Figure 1.3). Activate/deactivate the options you require or do not require. Click **OK** to confirm.

Help

You can also use the Help menu and Help toolbar icon to obtain help.

The options and the look you specify for the Office Assistant will apply to all Office applications.

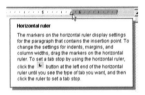

Figure 1.4 The ScreenTip describes the item you have just selected.

Context help

Context help is a help option that matches the context in which you are working; you can also get help for a command, a button, and so on.

To obtain Context help, open the Help Menu and select **What's This?** The pointer becomes a question mark. Click on the button or the command for which you require help. A ScreenTip is displayed, which describes the command or button (Figure 1.4).

To obtain Context help in a dialog box, click on the ? in the box, then on the button or the command for which you require help.

Help icons

To open the Help summary, click on the **?** in the tool bar, or select Microsoft Help from the **Help** menu. A window opens on the right-hand side of the screen.

■ The **Contents** tab displays a list of topics. Double-click on a topic to display it.

  ▧ A closed book next to a topic indicates that it contains a list of detailed icons. Double-click on it to open the list.

■ An open book next to a topic indicates that it is selected. Double-click on it to close the topic.

■ A question mark next to a section icon indicates that there is detailed text about this topic. To open it, double-click on the question mark or the topic label.

■ The **Index** tab allows you to search a topic based on the command name. In the **Type keywords** box, type the text corresponding to the command you require. Box 3 displays a list of icons concerning the entered text. To display the topic that corresponds to your search, click on it in box 3: the topic is displayed on the right-hand side of the window.

■ The **Answer Wizard** tab allows you to refine your search for Help. Type a word corresponding to the topic you are looking for in the **What would you like to do?** box. The outcome of the search is displayed in the **Select topic to display** area. Double-click on the topic of your choice in the second box.

*To print a Help topic, display it, then click on **Print** in the toolbar.*

Wizards and templates

Office XP contains a number of wizards and templates that you can use to speed up your work.

Templates

A template (with the .dot extension in Word) is a default document into which you simply insert your text.

To select a template, click on **File, New** then click on a Templates option in the Task Pane (Figure 1.5). The various tabs in the **New** dialog box offer several templates.

Figure 1.5 The tabs in the New dialog box allow you to select a template.

Click on the tab that corresponds to your requirements, then double-click on the template you wish to use.

To work with a template (Figure 1.6), you usually just need to modify the various text boxes. For example, in the **Click here and type name** text box of the Letter template, click on the text and type the required name. Before printing the template, just follow all the instructions. The boxes containing instructions will not be printed.

Wizards

A wizard is a sequence of dialog boxes where you specify your choice corresponding to the processing of a personal document.

To select a wizard, click on **File, New**. The tabs in the New dialog box offer several wizards. Click on the tab that corresponds to your requirements, then

You can also access the choice of templates by clicking on the **New Office document** *button in the Office Manager Shortcut bar.*

Figure 1.6 A letter template.

*When, in a wizard, you have clicked on the **Finish** button, you will not be able to go back.*

double-click on the wizard you wish to use. After completing each stage, click on the **Next** button to move to the next stage. If you make a mistake, or you wish to modify one of your choices, don't panic: click on the **Back** button. Once you have finished the procedures, click on the **Finish** button and the document will be displayed on the screen. You can implement customised formats by following the procedures included in the first chapters for each program.

Creating a template

Although there are several templates available, you may not find exactly what you are looking for. The solution? Create one!

To create a template:

1. In the application, click on **File, New** and select a New form template option in the Task Pane. In the **Create New** area (underneath the **Preview** area), click on the **Template** option and then on **OK**.

2. Create the document template, specifying the margins and the styles you require. When you have finished, click on **File, Save As**. You can also click on the **Save** icon in the Standard toolbar.

3. In the dialog box, type the name of your template in the **Name** box, then click on **Save** (Figure 1.7).

The application adds the template you have created to the existing ones. Whenever you wish to use it, simply select it in the **New** dialog box.

*When you save a template in the **Save As** dialog box, check that the **Save As type** box displays Document Template. If this is not the case, click on the **Up One Level** button (the icon of a folder with an upwards point-ing arrow), then select Document Template.*

Spelling and grammar

Office XP allows you to check spelling and grammar for documents, presentations, worksheets, and so on.

Automatic spellchecking

You can ask the application in which you are working to flag possible spelling errors. Click on **Tools, Options**, then click on the **Spelling & Grammar** tab and then the **Check spelling as you type** option (Figure 1.8). Click on **OK** to confirm.

Once this option has been activated, everything the software thinks is an error will be underlined with a wavy red line (Figure 1.9).

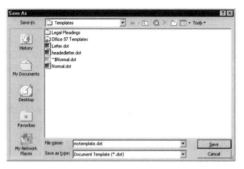

Figure 1.7 Enter the name of your template.

Figure 1.8 Activate the spellchecker as you type.

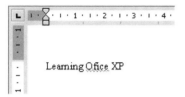

Figure 1.9 Spelling mistakes are underlined with a wavy red line.

To correct spelling errors, right–click on the underlined word, then select an option in the context menu.

- To select a word for correction, click on it.
- To add this word to the Office dictionary, click on **Add**.
- To ignore the error and to make sure that it is no longer shown as an error in the document, click on **Ignore All**.
- To choose another language, select **Tools, Language, Set Language**.

Automatic grammar check
You can ask the application in which you are working to flag possible grammatical errors. Click on **Tools, Options**, then click on the **Spelling & Grammar** tab and click on the **Check grammar as you type** option. Click on **OK** to confirm.

Once this option has been activated, everything the software thinks is a grammatical error will be underlined with a wavy green line.

*If you have chosen not to activate automatic spelling and grammar checking, you can still check your documents with the **Spelling & Grammar** option in the **Tools** menu. Spelling errors will be highlighted for you to correct.*

To correct grammar errors, follow the same procedure as for spelling.

Activating a language

In Office XP, French, English and Spanish are recognised by default by the spellchecker. Therefore, when you need to correct a text written, for example, in French, the words will not all be underlined as errors. Only actual French errors will be identified and the correction context menu will suggest the correct spelling. The available languages are marked with an ABC icon next to them in the list.

You can also activate other languages. In any of the Office applications, click on **Tools, Language, Set Language** (Figure 1.10). Select the language you wish to add from the list and click on **OK**.

Figure 1.10 Activate other languages.

AutoCorrect

When you start working in an application, you will notice that when you enter text, some misspelt words are corrected immediately. For example, if you have typed the word 'accomodate', this is automatically replaced with 'accommodate'. Furthermore, if you forget to start a sentence with a capital letter, the software replaces your lower-case letter with a capital. This is the AutoCorrect function. A list of words has been created in all office applications which tells the application how these should be spelt.

The list of misspelt words with their corresponding correct versions is not static: you can easily add your own corrections to it.

*If this option is not active, click on **Tools, AutoCorrect**. In the AutoCorrect tab, tick/clear the required options, then click on **OK**.*

To widen the scope of the AutoCorrect function:

1. Click on **Tools, AutoCorrect** (Figure 1.11).
2. Type the misspelt word in the **Replace** box. Press the **Tab** key to move to the **With** box, then type the correct word. Click on **Add** to confirm this creation.
3. Click on **OK** to close the dialog box. You can create as many automatic corrections as you want.

To delete an automatic correction, open the AutoCorrect dialog box. Select the word to be deleted in the list, then click on the **Delete** button. Then click on **OK**.

Find and Replace

So what happens if you have used a wrong word throughout a document? This is not difficult to correct manually if the document is only a few lines long, but if the document runs over several pages, Office suggests a better solution: the

*The **Exceptions** button in the AutoCorrect dialog box allows you to specify exceptions for some corrections.*

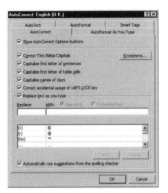

Figure 1.11 The AutoCorrect dialog box allows you to specify your correction parameters.

Find and **Replace** functions. Find allows you to search the whole document for the required word; Replace replaces the required word with a different one.

To find and replace a word or a group of words:

1. Go to the beginning of the document by pressing the **Ctrl+Home** keys.
2. Click on **Edit, Find**, then click on the **Replace** tab (Figure 1.12).
3. Type the word or group of words you wish to replace in the **Find what** text box. Type the word or group of words to replace this text within the **Replace with** text box. You can refine your replacement by clicking on the **More** button. To start the search, click on the **Find Next** button.

The first instance of the word you are looking for is displayed and highlighted.

Figure 1.12 You can replace text quickly and easily with Find and Replace.

4. Click on one of the proposed buttons remembering that:
   (a) **Find Next** goes to the next instance and ignores the selected one.
   (b) **Replace** replaces the selected instance of the find criteria, finds the next occurrence and then stops.
   (c) **Replace All** replaces all instances of the find criteria in your document.
   (d) **Cancel** closes the dialog box without saving any changes you have made.
   (e) **Close** closes the dialog box and retains the changes you have made.

Finding synonyms

When you proofread your document, you may well find that the same word has been used too frequently. It would be better to find a synonym.

To find a synonym for a word, select the word, then click on **Tools, Language**. In the drop-down menu, select **Thesaurus** (Figure 1.13). (You can also press the **Shift+F7** keys to do this). In the **Replace with Synonym** box there will be a list of words or expressions suggested as synonyms. In the

Meanings box you can see the various dictionary meanings of the selected word. Choose a synonym and click on the **Replace** button.

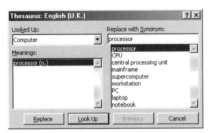

Figure 1.13 The Thesaurus allows you to search for synonyms.

Office XP and the Web

We will not launch into a long-winded explanation of how to use the Web and how useful it is, as there are several other books dealing specifically with this subject (e.g. *Internet* and *Internet Explorer 5* also available from Prentice Hall).

Office XP comes with Internet Explorer 5.5, a Web browser. When you installed Office, this navigator was also installed. If you have a modem and an Internet connection, you can connect directly to the Web from Office.

Browsing the Web from Office

If you have a connection to an Internet Service Provider (ISP) and are using Microsoft Internet Explorer as your browser, you can open Web pages directly from the Office applications with the Web toolbar. To display this toolbar, right-click on one of the active toolbars, then click on **Web** (Figure 1.14). Then use the various buttons to carry out the operation you wish to execute.

Figure 1.14 The Web toolbar.

To access a discussion group from one of the Office applications, click on **Tools, On-line Collaboration, Web Discussions**. Select the news server of your choice and get on-line.

Opening documents in Internet Explorer

The compatibility of Office functions with Internet Explorer allows all data in the browser to be retrieved once a document has been translated to HTML format. This means that the complexity of PivotTables will be no problem for the browser: it will retain the original formatting of the document!

To open a document in Internet Explorer once it has been saved in HTML format, click on **File, Open**. Select a file, then click on **Open**.

Web preview

Once a document or a presentation has been saved in HTML format, you can view it in a Web preview so that you can see exactly what your document will look like when it is published on the Web.

See p.28 to learn more about how to save a document to HTML format.

To display a Web preview for a document or a presentation, click on **File, Web Page Preview**.

On-line collaboration

To implement an on-line collaboration from one of the Office applications, simply connect to the Internet. Then, click on **Tools, On-line Collaboration, Meet Now**. Select the server name in the relevant option box. Netmeeting is launched and you can start to chat.

E-mailing from an application

You can now send a document by e-mail from any Office application. Use the **E-mail** button, accessible from the Standard toolbar in all the applications. Once this command is active, the editing window for the message is displayed (see Chapters 7 and 8). Get information on the various options, then send your message.

Creating hyperlinks

A Web page is not complete unless it has hyperlinks. A hyperlink allows you to direct the visitor, with a simple click, to another part of the page or to another site. All Office XP applications have an icon that allows you to insert hyperlinks to other documents, files or pages.

 To quickly change a standard text into a hyperlink:

1. Select the text, then click on the **Insert Hyperlink** button in the Standard toolbar (Figure 1.15).
2. Specify the URL (Web address) of the page to which the link goes. Type the hyperlink name in the **Type the file or Web page name** option, or select

the address in the list, or click on the **File** button, then select the file to which the hyperlink is directed. Click on **OK**.

Top marks for PowerPoint. Its XP version allows you to automatically create a resumé to the left of the site. Once you have displayed the presentation in the navigator, simply click on one of the points you wish to be included in the resume to display its contents directly in the window on the right (see Chapters 7 and 8).

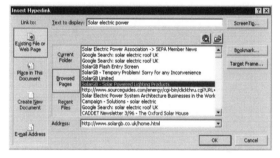

Figure 1.15 The Inset Hyperlink dialog box.

Shared commands

In this chapter we will look at the functions and commands shared by all Office applications.

Starting and quitting applications

When you have installed Office, the names of the various applications are placed in the **Start** menu in **Programs**.

Launching an application

To launch an application, click on **Start, Programs**, and then the relevant application (Figure 2.1). You can also open an application by clicking on the corresponding button in the Office shortcut bar.

The other solution is to place shortcut icons on your Windows Desktop. This function is useful for common applications: you simply double-click on the icon to quickly launch the program.

To create a program shortcut icon, click on **Start, Programs**. Click with the right mouse button on the program of your choice then, keeping the button pressed, drag it on to the Desktop. In the context menu, select **Create Shortcut**.

Quitting an application

To close a program, several solutions are offered:

- Click on **File, Close**. If a file is open, you will be asked whether you wish to save it. Click on **Yes** or **No**.
- Click on the **system** box, at the top left of the screen, which displays the program icon, then click on the **X** (Close).
- Press the **Alt+F4** keys.

Figure 2.1 Start the application of your choice with **Start, Programs**.

Undoing and redoing actions

The Undo and Redo functions allow you to undo or redo the action or the command you have just executed.

 Clicking on this button undoes the last action. If you wish to undo several actions, click on the small arrow and select all that you wish to undo. You can also click on **Edit, Undo [name of action]**.

*If you wish to repeat your last action, press **F4**.*

 Click on this button to redo the last action you have just undone. If you wish to redo several actions, click on the small arrow and select all that you wish to redo. You can also click on **Edit, Redo [name of action]**.

Interface elements

All the elements in this section are shared by all the applications running under Windows 95 and 98. It is not our intention here to show you the procedures for using your system, but you should be acquainted with some basic principles.

Menu bar

The Menu bar is positioned underneath the Title bar. Each menu (File, View, and so on) opens a drop-down list that offers several commands (Figure 2.2). Menus follow a number of parameters:

- Greyed commands are not available; commands in black are available.
- An arrowhead next to a command indicates that the command has a drop-down sub-menu.
- An ellipsis (...) after a command indicate that the command opens a dialog box that allows you to select options, specify choices, and so on.
- A button positioned in front of a command indicates that the command can also be found as a shortcut in one of the toolbars.
- A key combination, such as **Ctrl** or **Alt** followed by a letter, displayed next to a command confirms that this command also has a keyboard shortcut. By pressing these keys, you will automatically open the command or its dialog box (for example, with the **Ctrl+P** keys, you open the Print dialog box).

Figure 2.2 The Menu bar in Word.

To make your tasks easier, the XP version allows automatic menu customisation. Therefore, while you work, menus are adapted to your choice and display only what you are using. To view a complete menu, simply click on the two arrowheads () at the bottom of the menu, or double-click on the menu name (for example, double-click on **File** to view the default menu).

Toolbars
Positioned underneath the Menu bar, toolbars allow quick access to some of the most commonly used commands. By default, programs display two toolbars: **Standard** and **Format**. However, you can display several others.

To display a toolbar, click with the right mouse button on a toolbar and select the required toolbar from the menu.

To hide a toolbar, right-click on a toolbar and click on the one you wish to hide.

The toolbar customisation options are very simple. To customise a toolbar once you have it on the screen:

1. Click with the right mouse button on any toolbar and, at the bottom of the drop-down toolbar menu, select **Customize**.

The Task Pane
Some of the more commonly-used operations that were previously handled by dialog boxes are now run in the Task Pane, an independent area of the screen to the right of the main working area. Unlike a dialog box, the Task Pane will remain open after you have completed the operation, allowing you to repeat the task without having to reopen a dialog box.

The **Back** *button is the same as the one used in Internet browsers.*

Toolbars take up little space because they can be displayed next to each other and they change according to the user's needs. To view the whole of a toolbar, simply click on the two right-pointing arrowheads on its right edge.

2. In the Customize dialog box, the **Options** tab allows you to specify the display (large icons, list of fonts, ScreenTips, and so on). The **Toolbars** tab allows a toolbar to be activated and new ones to be created, while the **Commands** tab lists the various categories of buttons as well as their icons.

3. To add an icon to a toolbar, select the category, click on the button to be added in the list on the right and drag it into the relevant toolbar. Click on **Close** to confirm.

To delete a button, click on the arrowheads in the relevant toolbar, select **Add/Remove** buttons (Figure 2.3), then click on the option check box against the command to be removed.

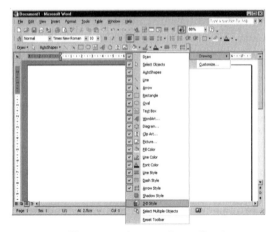

Figure 2.3 You can easily turn off a toolbar button.

Saving data

To save a document, worksheet or slide, simply click on the **Save** button in the Standard toolbar or click on **File, Save**. The procedure is very different depending on whether you are saving the file for the first or the nth time.

To save a file for the first time:

1. Click on the **Save As** command in the File menu (Figure 2.4).
2. Select the folder in the **Save in** area or use the Views bar by clicking on the folder (for example **My Documents**).
3. Type the name of the file to be saved in the **File name** box (do not type the extension; this is generated automatically by the application from which you are saving). Click on the **Save** button.

When you save the document the next time, simply click on the **Save** button in the Standard toolbar.

Figure 2.4 The Save As dialog box.

Saving documents in HTML format

The HTML format is the format used on the Web. Regardless of the document you wish to publish (text, presentation, worksheet, and so on), you must change it to an HTML document before publishing it. Without this transformation, it will not be readable on the Web.

To save a document or a presentation to HTML format:

1. Click on **File, Save as Web Page**.
2. Name the file in the **Name** box. You can edit its title by clicking on the **Change Title** button. Click on **OK** in the **Set Page Title** box (Figure 2.5), then on **Save**.

Figure 2.5 Changing the name of your Web page.

Saving on a server

To save a document on a Web server, click on **File, Save as Web Page**. In the Views bar, click on **Web Folders**, which contain possible shortcuts to the Web server(s). Select the server of your choice. Name the document and click on **Save**.

File management

The concept of file management will be familiar to you if you have some experience in using computers. If you are a beginner, here are some explanations. In Windows,

You can save a document directly on to a server, for example on your company's intranet.

when you create a document, table, presentation, and so on, you create a file. Files are kept in folders. You can see all the files in your computer in Explorer.

Opening files

To open a file, click on the **Open** button in the Standard toolbar or on **File, Open** (Figure 2.6). Select the folder that contains the required file in the **Look in** box, or use the Views bar. Then simply double-click on the file.

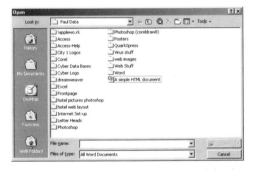

Figure 2.6 Opening a file in the Open dialog box.

*To open a recently opened file, click on **File**: the file is displayed at the bottom of the menu; simply click on it to open it. If the program is not open, you can also click on **Start, Documents**. A list of the last 15 files used is displayed. Select the one you wish to open.*

Closing files

To close a file, either click on the **Close** window button (shown by an X), or click on **File, Close**.

Deleting and renaming files

To delete a file, click on the **Open** button. In the dialog box, click with the right mouse button on the relevant file and select **Delete**. Click on **Yes** to confirm the deletion.

To rename a file, click on the **Open** button. In the dialog box, click with the right mouse button on the relevant file and select **Rename**. Type the new name and press **Enter** to confirm.

Printing

First, switch on your printer, then click on the **Print** button. Or, if you wish to specify the printer to be used, the number of copies to be made, and so on, click on **File, Print**, then specify your choice in the Print dialog box (Figure 2.7). Click on **OK** to confirm your choice and start printing.

Cut, copy, paste and move

When creating documents, you may need to move, cut or copy a word, sentence or object. These procedures are very simple.

To copy, select the element you want, then press the **Ctrl+C** keys. You can also click on **Edit, Copy**.

To cut, select the relevant element, then press the **Ctrl+X** keys. You can also click on **Edit, Cut**.

To paste an item, press the **Ctrl+V** keys. You can also click on **Edit, Paste**.

To move, select the item on your document, then click on the selection. Keeping the mouse button pressed, drag it to where you wish to move it to. Release the mouse button.

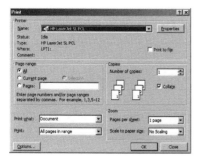

Figure 2.7 The Print dialog box in Word.

You can also use the **Copy, Cut** or **Paste** buttons. Their procedures are identical to those we have just seen.

The Office Clipboard

In previous versions of Office, when you copied or cut an item, the action automatically deleted the previous Clipboard contents. This is no longer the case. Now, you can store up to 24 items in the Clipboard. When you wish to paste an element, simply select it in the Clipboard.

When you cut and/or copy several items, the Clipboard is displayed in the Task Pane automatically (Figure 2.8). Position your cursor where you wish to insert one of these items. Click on the item of your choice in the Clipboard display: the item will be inserted in the document.

If you click **Paste All**, all the items in the Clipboard will be pasted at the cursor position. Use this for reorganising text.

*When you copy or cut a piece of text or an object with the **Edit**, **Copy** or **Edit**, Cut commands, the element is stored in the **Clipboard**, which is a sort of waiting room. You can then paste the contents of this Clipboard into another document or page.*

*If the Clipboard toolbar is not displayed, right-click button on a toolbar and select **Clipboard**.*

Figure 2.8 The Clipboard toolbar.

Inserting text styles

With WordArt, you can produce texts that stretch or curve, create angles or even display characters in 3D.

To insert a WordArt text object:

1. Click on where you wish to place the text then click on **Insert, Picture, WordArt** (Figure 2.9).

2. Click on the style, then confirm by clicking on **OK**.

3. A new dialog box is displayed. Enter the text to which the selected style will be applied; make your formatting choices, such as font, size, attributes, and so on, then click on **OK**.

The text is inserted in the document (Figure 2.10).

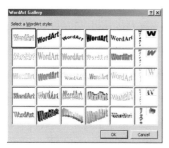

Figure 2.9 The WordArt sub-application allows you to create titles.

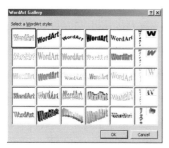

Figure 2.10 Place WordArt text to add the finishing touches to a document.

Moving, resizing, copying and deleting a WordArt object

A text created with WordArt corresponds to a graphic object: when you select it, it becomes surrounded by small squares known as 'handles', which allow the object to be moved, resized, and so on.

To move a WordArt object, click on it. Then, keeping the button pressed, drag it to where you wish it to go and release the button.

To cut, copy or paste a WordArt object, use the Cut, Copy or Paste commands in the Edit menu, or use the corresponding buttons.

To resize the WordArt object, click on one of its handles and drag it in the required direction.

To delete a WordArt object, click on it to select it, then press the delete key.

WordArt toolbar

The WordArt toolbar, which is displayed when you select the text object, allows you to modify and format the object. Table 2.1 shows the various buttons and their functions.

Table 2.1 WordArt toolbar buttons

Button	Action
	Inserts a new WordArt object into the page.
Edit Text...	Modifies the text of the WordArt object.
	Selects another style for the WordArt object.
	Modifies size, position and colour for the object, and places the text around it.
Abc	Selects another shape for the WordArt object.
	Defines text wrapping.
Aa	Sets all the object characters at the same height.
	Displays characters vertically.
	Modifies text alignment.
AV	Modifies character spacing in the WordArt object.

Copying a format

Not only is formatting characters quick and easy in Office; it is also possible to copy the various formatting choices.

 To reproduce a format, select the word or the sentence, then click on the **Format Painter** button on the Standard toolbar. The pointer becomes a paintbrush. Drag the paintbrush on to the word or the sentence in which you wish to copy the format. Release the button. To copy the formatting to more than one item, double-click and then click on each item you want to format. When you are finished, press **Esc** or click again to turn off the Format Painter.

Inserting pictures

Office allows you to insert pictures into any document. Pictures come ready-made on the Media Content CD, which also contains sound files and animated clips.

Inserting a personal picture

When you insert pictures into a document, you will make the document easier to understand and, above all, more original. You can insert a picture that you have scanned, or even one you have found on the Web.

To insert a picture that you have saved:

1. Click on **Insert, Picture, From File**.
2. Select the type of graphic file you wish to insert. Select the folder that contains the file. For the picture to be inserted into your page, double-click on the file that contains it.

Insert a clip art picture

Office XP is supplied with a vast number of clip art pictures that you can insert into any documents.

To insert a clip art picture

1. Use **Insert, Picture, Clip Art...** to open **Insert Clip Art** in the Task Pane.
2. Type a word or words to describe the required picture into the **Search For** box.
3. Click the down arrow to open the **Results should be** list and tick the types of media that you want.
4. Click Search.
5. Scroll through the results to find a picture.
6. To insert it, double-click or click the arrow bar and select **Insert**.

Figure 2.11 Preparing to insert from the Task Pane.

See Chapters 7 and 8 for further information on how to edit a picture.

Figure 2.12 Selecting a picture from the results. If you do not see what you want, click Modify to try a search using different words.

Clip Organizer

The Clip Organizer can help you to keep track of your clip art, video and sound clips, pictures, photographs – in fact, just about any type of multimedia file. The Organizer can be opened from the link at the bottom of the Task Pane

When first installed, the Clip Organizer only knows about the media files on the Office CD. These are organised into collections – which is just as well as there are thousands of them! Browse through the collections as you would browse through the folders on a disk.

When you have time, explore its options. You can create new collections of your own, and add your own files to the collections.If you have more than a few images on your computer, do not ask the Organizer to search your hard drive and add the images automatically. They will all go into one huge collection which will be hard to manage.

Figure 2.13 Browsing files in the Clip Organizer. There are countless numbers of files in the Office XP set.

The Web is a gold mine for those who need pictures. In fact, there are thousands of sites where you can retrieve pictures to use in a document.

To find a picture on the Web:

1. Open ClipArt. Click on the **Clips On-line** button in the toolbar. Obviously, you must first be connected to the Internet.
2. In the dialog box click on **OK**: the navigator is launched. Surf the Web. In the site that contains the picture you like, select the picture: this is then inserted automatically into ClipArt.

Pictures downloaded from a site that is not in the public domain cannot be used for commercial purposes.

Basic Word functions

3

In this chapter, you will learn about basic Word functions, including entering text, formatting it, and modifying the page view.

Creating a new document

By default, when you launch Word, a blank document and the Office Assistant are displayed.

To open a blank document, click on the **New** button. You can also click on **File, New** then click on **Blank Document** in the Task Pane.

Figure 3.1 Opening a new document.

The Word screen

Before going any further, let us examine the Word screen and its various items (Figure 3.2). From the Menu bar you can access all the Word function; the various toolbars offer shortcut buttons for more frequently used commands or functions. The flashing cursor is the default insertion point for your text. Scroll the vertical or horizontal scroll bar to move within the page.

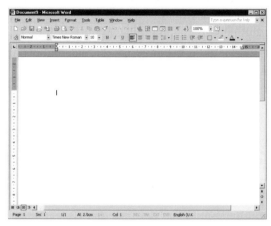

Figure 3.2 The Word screen.

Entering text

Here are some rules and tips you should know when entering text:

- By default, the flashing cursor, or insertion point, shows where the text will be entered.

- Word automatically goes on to a new line when you reach the right margin.

- To create a new paragraph, press the **Enter** key. Also use this procedure to insert a blank line.

- To go to a new line without creating a new paragraph, press the **Shift+Enter** keys.

- At the bottom of the page, the horizontal line marks where the page ends. If you wish to insert text beyond this line, Word automatically creates another page. To insert a forced page break, press **Ctrl+Enter**.

- Avoid using the Tab key to create indents in the text. It is better to do this with the **Indent** keys.

When you create paragraphs or insert blank lines, Word generates characters known as 'non-printing characters'. To view them, click on the button that displays the **Show/Hide formatting marks** symbol in the Standard toolbar. You can also click on **Tools, Options**. In the **View** tab, click on the icon in the **Formatting marks area**, then click on **OK** to confirm your choice.

Non-breaking hyphens, non-breaking spaces and accented upper case
When typing, Word automatically wraps text over on to new lines. If a word should not be split over two lines, you must create a non-breaking space or a nonbreaking hyphen.

To create a non-breaking space, type the first word, then press **Ctrl+Shift+Spacebar**. Type the second word and again press **Ctrl+Shift+Spacebar**.

To create a non-breaking hyphen, type the first word, press **Ctrl+Shift+the hyphen key**, then type the second word.

When you type titles or any other text in upper case, Word does not display accents. For more sophisticated entry, you can create titles with accented upper-case characters.

To insert accented upper-case characters:

1. Click on **Insert, Symbol** (Figure 3.3).
2. Click on the character you wish to insert. Click on the **Insert** button, then on the **Close** button.

Figure 3.3 Use Symbols for accented capital letters.

Moving within the text

To move within the text:

■ Point to where you want to be, then click.

- Scroll the vertical or horizontal scroll bar in the direction of your choice (up, down, left or right). A little box will appear: this shows the number of the page that will be displayed if you release the mouse.

- Click on the **Previous Page** or the **Next Page** arrows to display the previous or the following page. These arrows are positioned at the bottom of the vertical scroll bar.

- Click on one of the arrows at the bottom of the vertical scroll bar to scroll the text up or down. Release the mouse button when the text is displayed.

Going to a specific page

To go to a specific page, click on **Edit, Go To** (Figure 3.4). Type the page number, then click on the **Go To** button. To go to a specific item in your document, in the **Go to what** list, click on the item, then enter the item number, and click on the **Go To** button. Click on the **Close** button.

Figure 3.4 Use the **Go To** tab to display a page or specific element.

Selecting text

For all text manipulations (moving, copying, deleting, formatting, and so on) you must first select your text. Selecting consists of marking the text on which you want to act. Selected text is shown as highlighted.

To select a word, click on the beginning of the word, then drag the mouse over it keeping the button pressed.

To select a group of words, click in front of the first word to be selected, press the **Shift** key then, keeping the mouse button pressed, use the arrow keys to reach the end of the group you want to select.

To undo a selection, click outside the selected item.

Correcting text

Once your text has been entered, you may want to insert, replace, or delete one or more words or characters:

- To insert a word or character into existing text, click where you want to insert it, then type the new word or character.
- To replace a word with another one, double-click on the word, then type the replacement word.
- To delete text, select it, then press the delete key.
- To clear text positioned before the insertion point, press the backspace key.
- To clear text positioned after the insertion point, press the delete key.

Views

When you launch Word, a new document is displayed. It corresponds to a page, but you can see only half of it. You are in Page Layout view, which is the default display view. When creating a document, you might want to modify the display of pages. Word has several options for viewing pages on the screen.

Display views

Each view allows the execution of a specific task. You can access these views by opening the **View** menu, then selecting the view to be activated. You can also use the views buttons in the bottom left corner of the document.

The display views buttons are:

- **Normal View**. Displays pages as a long text divided into pages by automatic page breaks (dotted lines). This mode is easy to use because it requires very little memory.

- **Web Layout View**. Shows the document as it would look when published on the Web.

- **Print Layout View**. Displays the document as it will appear when printed. This view, which takes up a lot of memory, slows down the scrolling of the document.

- **Outline View**. Allows you to display the structure of your document, giving you the chance to modify it (Figure 3.5).

Zoom

The Zoom option allows you to modify the size of the page on the screen. To modify the amount of the zoom, click on the arrow in the **Zoom** drop-down list,

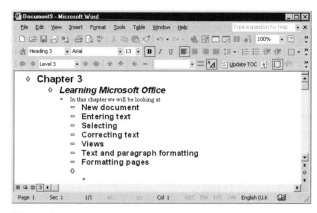

Figure 3.5 A document in Outline View.

then select the display percentage. You can also double-click on the text box, enter the percentage and press **Enter** to confirm.

Switching between several documents
It is possible to work simultaneously on several different documents.

To switch between various documents, click on **Window**. At the bottom of the menu, the list of open documents is displayed. Click on the document you wish to display.

To display several documents on the screen, click on **Window, Arrange All** (Figure 3.6).

Figure 3.6 You can display several documents on screen at the same time.

Formatting text and paragraphs

The Word default font is Times New Roman, 10 points, without attributes; paragraphs are left-aligned and have no indent.

Formatting procedures

You can define the format for characters and paragraphs before or after entry:

- **Format before entry**. Select the various formats as explained in this chapter, then type the text.

*A paragraph is a set of characters that finishes with a carriage return executed with the **Enter** key.*

- **Format after entry**. Select the text, then choose the various formats required.

Quick character formatting

The simplest and quickest method to format characters is to use the Format toolbar. Table 3.1 shows the various formats. Some of the buttons displayed on the Format toolbar are not included in this table: see p.52 to learn about them.

Table 3.1 Buttons for formatting characters in the Format toolbar

Button	Action
	Modifies font.
	Modifies text size.
	Makes text bold.
	Makes text italic.
	Underlines text.
	Selects highlight colour.
	Selects font colour.

To format a single word, there is no need to select it: simply click on it, then choose the various formatting options.

To delete a format, select the relevant text, then click on the attribute to deactivate it.

Sophisticated character formatting

The Font dialog box allows you to select all the character format options.

To use the Font dialog box (Figure 3.7), click with the right mouse button on the text to be formatted and choose **Font**. Carry out your format choice, then click on **OK**.

This is what can be done in the other tabs in the Font dialog box:

- **Character Spacing**. Allows you to modify spaces between characters.
- **Text Effects**. Allows you to animate the text, for example, by adding flashing lights round it. This function is important only if you are transferring your document as a file rather than as hard copy.

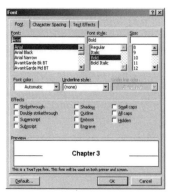

Figure 3.7 The Font dialog box allows you to select all the options for character formatting.

To modify the character case, click on **Format, Change Case** (Figure 3.8). Select the required option, then click on **OK**.

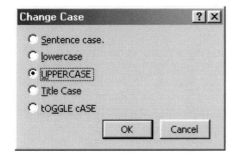

*The **tOGGLE cASE** option allows you to display in upper case text that was in lower case, and vice versa.*

Figure 3.8 The Change Case dialog box offers several options.

Quick paragraph formatting

The simplest and quickest method to format paragraphs is to use the Format toolbar. Table 3.2 shows the various formats.

Table 3.2 Buttons for formatting paragraphs in the Format toolbar

Button	Action
	Aligns the paragraph flush with the left margin.
	Centres the paragraph between left and right margins.
	Aligns the paragraph flush with the right margin.
	Spreads the text in the paragraph over the whole width of the page, between left and right margins.
	Creates a numbered list.
	Creates a bulleted list.
	Decreases the value of the paragraph indent in relation to the left margin.
	Increases the value of the paragraph indent in relation to the left margin.
	Frames a paragraph.

To delete a paragraph format, select the paragraph, then click on the relevant button to deactivate it in the Format toolbar.

Sophisticated paragraph formatting

The Paragraph dialog box allows you to select all the paragraph format options.

To use the Paragraph dialog box (Figure 3.9), click with the right mouse button on the text selected for formatting and choose **Paragraph**. Execute your formatting choices, then click on **OK**.

Figure 3.9 The Paragraph dialog box allows you to select paragraph formatting options.

This is what the Paragraph dialog box allows you to do:

■ **Indents and Spacing**. Allows you to modify paragraph alignment, indents and spacing. Alignment allows you to define the position of paragraphs in relation to the margins (Figure 3.10). Indents apply either to the whole of the paragraph, or to its first line (Figure 3.11); they allow you to indent the text in relation to the left margin. You can also modify indents with the ruler (Figure 3.12).

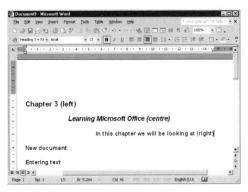

Figure 3.10 The various ways of aligning text.

Figure 3.11 Examples of indents.

First line indent | Hanging indent | Left indent

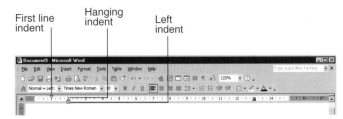

Figure 3.12 Using indents on the ruler.

■ **Line and Page Breaks**. Allows you to define the position of the paragraph in relation to other paragraphs. For example, you can request that the paragraph is not split at the end of the page.

*To undo paragraph formats and go back to the default options, select the relevant paragraph then press **Ctrl+Q**.*

Bulleted lists

To quickly create a bulleted list, use the **Numbering** or **Bullets** buttons in the Formatting toolbar (Table 3.2). When you click on one of these buttons, Word inserts a number or a bullet. Each time you enter an item in the list, simply click on **Enter** and the next number or a new bullet will appear. When you have finished entering the bullet list, press the backspace key or click on the relevant button in the Formatting toolbar to deactivate it.

You can modify the bullet or the type of number displayed in the bullet list.

To modify bullets or numbers:

1. Click with the right mouse button on the bullet list and select **Bullets and Numbering** (Figure 3.13).

Figure 3.13 The Bullets and Numbering dialog box allows you to modify numbered and bullet lists.

2. Click on the tab corresponding to your choice (**Bulleted** or **Numbered**). Click on the type of bullet or number you want. The **Customize** button allows you to select other types of bullets. Click **OK** to confirm your choice.

Borders and shading

The Borders and Shading functions allow you to frame a paragraph and to display it in varying shades of grey.

To create the border and the shading for a paragraph:

To delete a border, click on **Format, Borders and Shading**. *Click on the* **Borders** *tab, then select* **None** *in the border style. Click on* **OK** *to confirm your choice.*

1. Select the paragraph, then click on **Format, Borders and Shading**. Click on the **Borders** tab (Figure 3.14).

2. Select the style for the border, then choose the settings. You can modify the colour and the width of the border. If you wish to colour the background of the paragraph, click on the **Shading** tab. Choose the fill colour and the shading pattern, then click on **OK**.

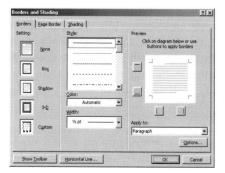

Figure 3.14 The Borders tab of the Borders and Shading dialog box.

Formatting pages

Word includes commands to enhance your page: you can frame the whole of a page, assign a coloured background or a picture background, and so on.

Framing a page
To frame your page, use the **Borders and Shading** function (see p. 56).

Background
You can assign a background to your page or to the whole document. The background will not print: it will be seen only in Web view. This function is therefore useful when you publish your document on your company's intranet or on the Web, or if you are going to send the document to someone on diskette or e-mail it.

*To delete a background, click on **Format, Background**. In the pop-down menu, click on **No Fill**.*

To choose a background, click on **Format, Background**. In the drop-down menu, click on the colour you want. The **More Colors** option opens a dialog box with two tabs: the **Standard** tab allows you to select another colour, and the **Custom** tab allows you to define the required colour by specifying the percentage for each component colour. If a simple background colour is not enough, click on the **Fill Effects** option. In the **Fill Effects** dialog box and its various tabs, you can choose gradient, texture (droplets, mosaic, and so on) and pattern. Click on **OK** to confirm your choices.

You can also opt for a picture as a background. This will appear as a watermark on the whole page. You have two possibilities: either use a picture from one of your files, or a ClipArt picture (see Chapter 2).

To choose a background picture:

1. Open the **Fill Effects** dialog box. Click on the **Picture** tab, then on the **Select Picture** button.
2. Select the file that contains the picture you wish to display as background. Click on **OK**.

Inserting a header and a footer

To insert a header or a footer, click on **View, Header and Footer**. A specific toolbar is displayed. The header will be shown framed by dots. Simply enter your wording, then use the various header and footer buttons in the toolbar to position it, for example, in the centre of the page.

Formatting

This is the last stage to complete before sending your document to print.

To execute formatting:

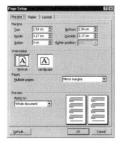

Figure 3.15 The Page Setup dialog box.

1. Click on **File, Page Setup** (Figure 3.15):
   (a) The **Margins** tab allows you to modify the margins for your document and to define gutters. In the Orientation area, you can set the document to be laid Portrait (vertical) or Landscape (horizontal). The **Mirror margins** option in the **Multiple pages** drop-down list is for recto–verso printing. The **Preview** area displays the defined choice. The **Apply to** option, by clicking on its arrow, opens a drop-down list in which you select the part of the document to which formatting applies.
   (b) The **Paper** tab allows you to set the size of the paper and to define the printer feed for this print job.
   (c) The **Layout** tab allows you to define the position of the text in your document (vertical or horizontal alignment) and to control the display of headers and footers. You can also choose to number lines in your document.
2. Click on the required tabs, then execute your choices.
3. Click on **OK** to confirm.

Advanced Word functions

Creating a table

Creating columns

Mailshots

Automatic format with styles

We have now reached the stage where we are able to look at more sophisticated functions in Word, such as creating tables, using mail merge, and so on.

Creating a table

*To customise rows and columns, use the **Tables and Borders** toolbar before drawing them.*

Whenever you have difficulties in aligning two text blocks or any other elements, you can use the Table function. A table is made up of rows and columns. Their intersections create cells.

Drawing a table

The Draw Table option allows you to create the general outline for your table. Once this is done, you split it into several parts by tracing lines and columns.

To draw a table:

*Use the eraser to clear incorrect rows or columns. The **Eraser** button is available in the Tables and Borders toolbar.*

1. Click on **Table, Draw Table**. The pointer becomes a pencil.
2. Click on the page where you wish to insert the table. Drag to draw a rectangle, which will form the frame for your table (Figure 4.1). Draw rows and columns to complete the table.
3. Once you have finished the 'drawing', click on **Table, Draw Table** so that the pointer goes back to its original shape.

Inserting a table

To quickly create a table, simply click on the **Insert Table** button: a little frame is displayed, which shows rows and columns for a table (Figure 4.2). Simply drag the mouse over it to select the number of rows and columns you require for the table. The textual description of the number of rows and columns selected is displayed at the bottom of this frame. Once you have finished, release the mouse. Word then inserts the table you have specified into the page.

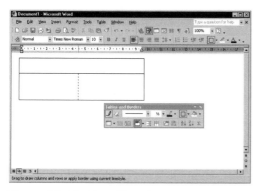

Figure 4.1 The Draw Table function allows you to create the outline for your table.

Figure 4.2 With the Insert Table button you can quickly create a table.

Table dialog box
The Table dialog box allows you to specify the number of rows and columns you want. You can assign up to 63 columns to a table.

Figure 4.3 You can specify the number of columns and rows in your table in the Insert Table dialog box.

To use the Table dialog box:

1. Click where you wish to insert the table, then click on **Table, Insert Table** (Figure 4.3).

2. Type the number of columns in the **Number of columns** box. Type the number of rows in the **Number of rows** box. In the **AutoFit behavior** area, select your choices. The **Auto** choice inserts columns of equal size between the document margins. The **AutoFormat** button automatically applies predefined formats to your table, including borders and shading.

3. Click on **OK** to confirm your choices.

The table defined in the dialog box will be shown in your document.

Moving within a table
Before entering data into the table, you must be able to move quickly within it. See Table 4.1 to see how you can achieve this.

Table 4.1 Moving within a table

To	Press
Go to the next cell	**Tab**
Go to the previous cell	**Shift+Tab**
Go to the first cell in the line	**Alt+Home**
Go to the first cell in the column	**Alt+PageUp**
Go to the last cell in the line	**Alt+End**
Go to the last cell in the column	**Alt+PageDown**

Table 4.2 The various selections in a table

To select	Procedure
A cell	Point towards the bottom left corner of the cell, then click.
A column	Point to the top border of the column, then click.
A row	Point to the left border of the row, then click.
The whole table	**Table, Select Table**.
The text of a following or previous cell	**Tab** or **Shift+Tab**.

Selecting within a table

Once your table has been created, you will be able to format it, add rows and columns, assign a border, and so on. To execute this formatting, you must know how to select the various items. Table 4.2 shows the selection procedures.

Inserting and deleting cells and rows

Once the table has been produced, you can edit it by deleting cells, adding rows, and so on.

To draw a table within a table, insert a table with the procedure shown above, then click on a cell and repeat the procedure – **Table, Insert Table** (Figure 4.4).

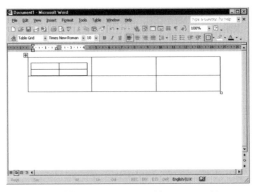

Figure 4.4 You can insert a table into a table.

To delete a cell, select it and press the delete key.

To insert a cell, select a cell, then click on **Table, Insert Cells** (Figure 4.5). Click on the option, then on OK.

Figure 4.5 You can insert a cell into a table.

To insert, for example, four rows, select four rows in the table, then click on the **Insert Rows** *button. Word automatically inserts four empty rows into the table.*

To insert a row, click on **Table, Insert Row**, then select the option. There is also a quicker method: click on the row below where you wish to insert the new row, then click on the **Insert Rows** button in the Tables and Borders toolbar.

To insert a column, select the column before the insertion, and click on the **Insert Columns** button in the Tables and Borders toolbar. You can also click on **Table, Insert Columns**.

To delete a row or a column, select it and press the delete key.

Orientation and display of the title row
You can change the orientation of text in cells. Click on the relevant cell, then on the **Change Text direction** button in the Tables and Borders toolbar.

When you create a table with several rows, not all the table will be visible on the screen. It is then difficult to enter text in the table: pretty soon, you start to get mixed up because you can't see the column headers. The best solution is to leave the title for all columns permanently displayed at the top of the page by selecting the title row then clicking on **Table, Titles**.

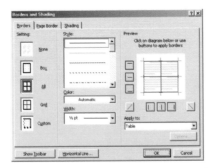

Figure 4.6 The Borders and Shading dialog box.

Formatting tables

To format a table – not the characters in the various cells – you can choose one of these methods:

■ **AutoFormat**. Select the table, and click on **Table, Table AutoFormat**. Select the template, then click on **OK**.

■ **Borders and Shading**. Select the table, and click on **Format, Borders and Shading**. Click on the **Borders** tab, then choose the border in the **Style** area (Figure 4.6). Click on the **Shading** tab if you wish to assign shading to the table. Define your choices, then click on **OK**.

Creating columns

There are two methods of creating columns. Click on the **Columns** button in the Standard toolbar, then select the number of columns you wish to apply.

The second method consists of clicking on **Format, Columns** (Figure 4.7), selecting the appropriate **Presets** option, and then clicking on **OK**.

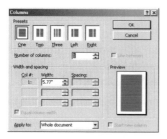

Figure 4.7 Choose the number of columns in the Columns dialog box.

Once you have created columns, simply insert your text with the following procedures:

- Just type away: Word automatically 'wraps' to the next line when you reach the end of the column.
- To go to the following column, click on **Insert, Break**, then select the type of break in the **Break** dialog box. The page break goes to the next page; the section break goes to the next column.

Mailshots

When you need to send an identical letter several people, use the Mail Merge function and its various elements:

Have you inserted a column break and now the columns are not balanced? To balance columns, insert a Continuous break.

- **Main document**. This is the basic document to which your variable data will be added when doing a mail merge. These data are placed in the relevant fields according to various criteria. This document contains the text that is common to all the letters you need to print, as well as the fields where the variables go when merging takes place.

- **Data source**. This is the document that contains all the variable data. The variable data are inserted into the relevant fields when merging takes place. It is the database to which the main document refers when printing the letters.

- **Merge fields**. These are areas in your main document where the data from the data source will go.

- **Merge**. This command allows you to create letters, and merges the main letter with the contents of the variable data source. Once this merge is executed, you can print your letters directly or display them on screen.

Main document

The first thing to do is to create the main mail merge document, i.e. the letter you are going to send to all the people included in your mailshot.

1. Open a blank document. Click on **Tools, Letters and Mailings, Mail Merge** to display the Mail Merge wizard in the Task Pane.

2. Select the type of document that you are working on, in this case Letters. Click the **Next** link at the bottom of the pane.

3. At the next step you will be asked if you wish to create your letter from the current document or if you wish to start one from a template to use an existing document. Select **Use the current document** and click the **Next** link.

Figure 4.8 The Mail Merge wizard makes it easy for you to choose and merge the elements of the mailshot.

4. At the **Select Recipients** step you can choose to use an existing list, type a new list or select from your Outlook contacts. Select **Type a new list** then click the **Create link** which will appear just below. The **New Address List** dialog box will open. Type the names and addresses of your recipients here, clicking **New Entry** after each one, and **Close** at the end. You will be prompted to save the list as a file. Give it a suitable name and click **Save**.

5. After you have created your address list, you will be shown the **Mail Merge Recipients** dialog box. You will also see this if you choose to use an existing list or your contacts. If there are any people on the list that you do not want to receive the mailing on this occasion, clear the tick box beside their name. Click **OK** to close the box, then click the **Next** link to move on.

*If the people that you want to mail to are in your contacts list, click the **Select from Outlook contacts** at the Select Recipients step. Initially, all the contacts will be selected. Rather than go through clearing the tick boxes for those that you do not want to include, you may find it simpler to click the **Clear All** button and then tick the ones you want.*

Figure 4.9 Adding a recipient to the address list. If you want to change the structure of the address fields, click Customize and add or remove fields as required.

6. At the **Write your letter** step, you should first write the standard text for the letter (if you have not already done so). Position the cursor where you want the recipient's address to go, then add the address fields. This can be done in two ways. The simplest is to use the **Address block** link. This will copy in the standard name and address fields, with their presentation tailored to suit your needs, in a single operation. If you do not want the standard set, then click the **More items** link and select the fields as required.

7. Place the cursor where you want the salutation and click the **Greeting line** link. A dialog box will open for you to set the style for the salutation.

8. Click Next: **Preview your letters**. You should have something along the lines of the one shown in Figure 4.11. View the previews for enough of the recipients to be sure that the merge document layout works well. If you need to adjust the layout, after inserting the fields, click the **Previous link** to return to the Write your letter step. If you have a fairly small recipient list, you might want to go through all of the recipients to make sure that you have everyone you should have (and no more).

Figure 4.10 Using the Insert Address Block dialog box is much simpler than inserting address fields by hand. Simply select the items to include, and decide on the style of the recipients' names, then click **OK**.

Figure 4.11 The main document with the merged address block and greeting line fields. If, when you preview the document, you decide you do not like the address block, you can return to this stage, delete the address block and use the More items routine to insert the fields separately.

Before you merge the main document with your address list, click the **Check for errors** button on the Mail Merge toolbar. At the Checking and Reporting Errors dialog box, select the **Simulate a merge** option and click **OK**. All being well, you should get a 'No mail merge' report; if not, the report will guide you to the source of the problem.

9. Click **Next: Complete** the merge. If you are confident that the merge needs no further work, make sure that your printer is on, click **Print**, select the records to print and set it off. If you need to do any further editing to letters, use the **Edit individual letters** options and edit and print each merged letter separately.

Automatic format with styles

A style is a set of formatting characteristics (size, alignment, attributes, and so on) that can be applied to a paragraph or character. This function means you do not have to repeat formatting instructions when the document contains several pages.

Choosing a style

Word offers a certain number of styles that you can apply to paragraphs or to characters.

To choose a style:

Some styles apply only to paragraphs, others only to characters.

1. Click in the relevant paragraph or select the required words. Click on the little arrow in the **Style** button (Figure 4.12).

2. Select the style.

   The paragraph is now displayed with the selected style attributes, and the **Style** button displays the active style in its text box.

Figure 4.12 You can quickly choose a style with the Style button.

Creating a style

Word offers a large variety of styles, but it is possible that none of them is suitable for one of your documents. In this case, you can create a personal style that you can then apply to all your documents.

To create a style, specify all the formatting (size, font, attributes, alignment, indent and so on) and click on the arrow in the **Style** button. Type the name of your new style and press **Enter**. The style that you have just specified is now an integral part of the styles for this document. To apply it to another paragraph, simply click on the relevant paragraph, then select the style of your choice in the drop-down list from the **Style** button.

If you cannot see the style that you need in the list, click the More link at the bottom to display styles and formatting in the Task Pane. Existing styles can be edited here.

Basic Excel functions

5

We will now look at the basic functions of Excel, including how to enter data, how to manage a workbook and its worksheets, the functions that help with entering data, and the various formatting procedures.

The first step

By default, when you launch Excel, a blank workbook is displayed. We have already seen how to open an existing workbook. To open a new workbook, simply click on the **New** button.

Screen

Before going any further, let us examine the screen and its various items (Figure 5.1). From the Menu bar you can access all the functionalities of Excel; the various toolbars offer shortcut buttons to the most frequently used commands or functions. The A1 cell (see below) is surrounded by a black frame, which indicates that it is selected.

Workbooks and worksheets

A workbook is made up of worksheets. By default, the workbook has three worksheets. Worksheets can be opened with the tabs positioned at the bottom of the workbook. Each worksheet is made up of little boxes known as cells. These are arranged to a maximum of 256 columns, named A to IV, and on 65 336 rows, named 1 to 65 336. Each cell has the name of the intersection between the row and the column where it is placed. For example, the A5 cell is at the intersection of the first column and the fifth row.

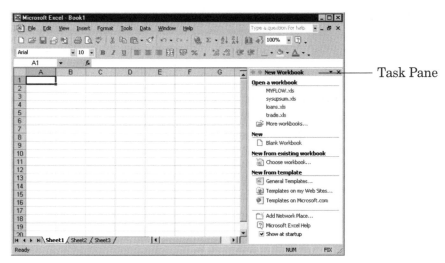

Task Pane

Figure 5.1 The Excel screen.

Worksheet management

Worksheets are the basic working tools. You should know how to move within them, how to add, delete, and so on.

Moving between worksheets

To move between worksheets or to select a specific one, use the tabs positioned at the bottom left of the screen. Here are some tips to speed up your work:

- To move between worksheets, use the scroll buttons positioned to the left of the tabs. The two middle buttons allow you to go back or forward by one tab; the left button goes back to the first tab; and the right button goes to the last one.

- Click with the right mouse button on one of the scroll buttons, then select the worksheet to be displayed (Figure 5.2).

- To select several worksheets, press the **Ctrl** key. Keeping it pressed, click on the tab of each worksheet to be selected.

Figure 5.2 Choose which worksheet to view in the context menu.

Adding, deleting, copying and moving worksheets

By default, a workbook offers three worksheets. Let us now see how to add, delete and move worksheets.

To add a worksheet, click on one of the tabs, then click on **Insert, Sheet**.

To delete a worksheet, click with the right mouse button on its tab, then select **Delete**. Confirm its deletion (Figure 5.3).

To move a worksheet within the workbook, click on its tab then, keeping the button pressed, drag it to the position of your choice.

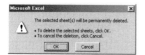

Figure 5.3 Confirm the deletion of the worksheet.

To copy a worksheet in its workbook, click on its tab, then keep the **Ctrl** key pressed and drag it to where you wish to place the copy.

To copy or move a worksheet to another workbook:

1. Open the two workbooks. Right-click on the tab of the worksheet you wish to move or copy. Select the **Move or Copy** option (Figure 5.4).

Figure 5.4 The Move or Copy dialog box allows you to specify the workbook into which you want to copy your worksheet.

2. Click on the arrow in the **To book** box. Select the workbook into which you wish to copy or move the selected worksheet.

3. In the **Before sheet** list, click on the worksheet in front of which you wish to position the new sheet tab. Click on **OK** to confirm your choice.

Hiding and showing a worksheet

You may wish to hide one of the sheets in a workbook; for example, if your PC is connected to your company's intranet, you may need to hide some data.

To hide a worksheet, select it and click on **Format, Sheet, Hide**.

To view a hidden worksheet, click on **Format, Sheet, Unhide**. In the dialog box (Figure 5.5), click on the worksheet you wish to display and click on **OK**.

Figure 5.5 View a hidden worksheet.

Your worksheets' names can be up to 31 characters long. However, it is better not to make names too long, as the name tab will take up too much space.

Naming, grouping and ungrouping worksheets

To name a worksheet, right-click on its tab, then select **Rename** (Figure 5.6). Type the new name and press **Enter**.

You can group worksheets together to speed up your work. This is the equivalent of inserting carbon paper between worksheets: everything you enter and

Figure 5.6 Renaming a worksheet.

format on the first worksheet is reproduced on the other worksheets in the group.

To group together several worksheets, click on the first tab of the group, keep the **Ctrl** key pressed, then click on the other tabs you wish to group.

To ungroup worksheets, click on one of the tabs that is not grouped.

Data

Before starting your calculations, you must enter data. Data for a worksheet can be numbers, legends or formulas.

Types of data
Excel allows the insertion of several types of data (Figure 5.7):

- **Numbers**. Raw data. These numbers are entered in cells.
- **Legends**. Text typed at the top of a column or the start of a row to specify its contents.
- **Formulas**. Entries that tell Excel which calculations to carry out. For example, the formula =A2-A5+B8 indicates to Excel that it must add cell A2 and B8, then subtract cell A5.

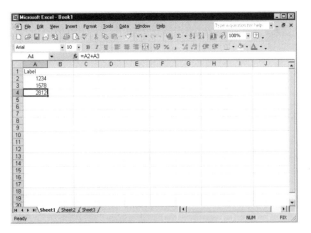

Figure 5.7 Excel allows you to enter several types of data.

■ **Functions**. Predefined formulas that execute more complex calculations with a single operator. For example, the **Average** function calculates the average for a set of values.

Excel applies a different alignment to cells according to the nature of the inserted data. Text is left-aligned, while numbers, functions, dates and formulas are right-aligned.

Entering data

To enter data, click on the relevant cell. A black frame will be shown around the cell to indicate that it is selected. As soon as you start entering data, it is displayed in the active cell and in the Formula bar (Figure 5.8). Click on the green box in the Formula bar to confirm the entry and insert it in the cell (you can also press **Enter**). Click on the red X to undo your entry (you can also press **Esc**).

Figure 5.8 You can insert, confirm and delete data in the Formula bar.

To edit the contents of the cell in which you are entering your data, use the backspace or delete keys, then type your correction. To edit the confirmed entry, double-click on the cell, then implement your correction. You can also click on the cell and edit its contents in the Formula bar.

Special data

As we have already said, text is left-aligned and values are right-aligned. However, in some cases you may wish to insert numbers as text (for example, a postcode). In such cases, you must tell Excel that this is text. Before starting your text entry, press the **apostrophe** (') key.

On the other hand, a date or a time, although it is text, must be considered as a value because it may be used for calculation purposes. To insert date or time values in a worksheet, enter them in the format you wish to be displayed (Table 5.1).

If your entry does not fit into the cell, the content is cut if it is text, or displayed as asterisks if it is a number when you confirm the entry. To fit the column automatically to its contents, click on **Format, Column** *and select* **AutoFit Selection**.

Table 5.1 Date formats

Entry	Outcome
DD/MM	1/1 or 01/01
DD/MM/YY	1/1/02 or 01/01/02
MMM-YY	Jan-02 or January-02
DD-MMM-YY	1-Jan-02
DD-MMM	1 January
DD Month YYYY	1 January 2002
HH:MM	17:15
HH:MM:SS	10:25:59
DD/MM/YY HH:MM	25/12/02 13:15

Selecting

These are the various selection procedures:

■ To select a cell, click on it.

■ To select a row, click on its number in the row header.

■ To select a column, click on its letter in the column header.

■ To select the whole worksheet, click on the greyed button at the intersection of a row header with a column header.

Cell range

You may need to select the same group of cells several times. To speed up the task, you can create a cell range:

- For a range with adjacent cells, click on the first cell, then drag the mouse to the last cell in the range.

- For a range with non-adjacent cells, click on the first cell, keep the **Ctrl** key pressed, click on the second cell, and so on.

To name a range:

1. After selecting a range, click on the reference, which is on the left-hand side of the Formula bar (Figure 5.9). Type the name following these rules:

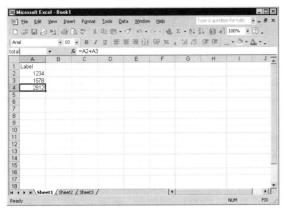

Figure 5.9 Naming a cell range in the reference box.

(**a**) The range name must start with a letter or an underscore.

(**b**) The range name must not be the reference for any cell.

(**c**) Do not use spaces between characters or digits.

(**d**) Use the underscore to separate two words.

(**e**) Type a maximum of 255 characters.

2. Press the **Enter** key.

Once you have named your range, to select it you simply click on **Edit, Go To** and specify the range you want (Figure 5.10).

Figure 5.10 Selecting a range in the Go To dialog box.

Managing cells, rows and columns

Sometimes you need to insert or delete cells, rows or columns.

To insert a cell, row or column, right-click on the cell before or after the place you wish to insert the new element, then select **Insert, Cells** (Figure 5.11).

Figure 5.11   You can insert cells, rows and columns using the Insert dialog box.

Click the choice you require, then click **OK**.

To delete one or more blank cells, rows or columns, after having selected them, right-click on the selection, then select **Delete**. You can also click on **Edit, Delete** (Figure 5.12). Select your choice from the list, then click on **OK**.

Figure 5.12   With the Delete dialog box, you can delete cells, rows and columns.

To delete only the text or the values from one or more cells, select the relevant cells, and press the delete key. The cells are kept, but their contents are deleted. On the other hand, if you wish to delete the contents of a formula, but not the format or the comments, select the formula, click on **Edit, Clear**, then select the appropriate option in the drop-down menu.

Remember that:

- **Contents** clears text from the cell.
- **Format** clears the format, but keeps the existing text.
- **Comments** clears the comments.
- **All** clears the set of choices defined above.

Help with your entry

Excel offers several functions to help you with entering data, which allow you to work faster.

Fill

To insert the same label value or date into several cells, use the **Fill** function.

To fill a value, date or label in the same worksheet:

*To copy one or more cells, you can also use the **Copy**, **Paste** or **Cut** buttons in the Standard toolbar.*

Figure 5.13 The Fill command.

1. Drag your mouse onto the cell that contains the entry for the fill, then onto those to which you wish to apply the fill. Click on **Edit, Fill**.

2. Select the direction for the fill – **Down, Right, Up, Left** (Figure 5.13).

   Excel fills the selected cells with the contents of the first cell.

Fill handles

To fill a cell, you can also use the fill handle (Figure 5.14). Before using this handle, make sure you are aware of all its different uses.

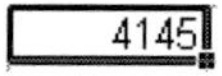

4145

Figure 5.14 A fill handle.

- A fill handle will be shown in a row header when you select it. Drag it to fill the contents of the row. Repeat this procedure in a column header to fill the whole column.

- To insert blank columns, rows or cells, press the **Shift** key, then drag the fill handle.

- Drag the fill handle with the right button to display its context menu.

To use a cell fill handle, click on the relevant cell. A little square is displayed on the bottom right corner: this is the fill handle. Click on it, then drag it on the cells to be filled.

According to the contents of the cell, Excel executes different types of fill:

- If the cell contains a numerical value, Excel fills this value.
- If the cell contains, for example, a month, Excel inserts the following month in sequence.

This function corresponds to inserting a series. Excel offers several integrated series in AutoFill. You can create your own fill series.

To create an automatic fill series:

1. Click on **Tools, Options**, then on the **Custom List** tab. If required, click on **NEWLIST** in the list on the left. Type the new list and click on the **Add** button.

2. Click on **OK** to confirm your automatic series.

Formatting

Excel offers several possibilities for formatting a table. You have the same choice of attributes (font, bold, italic, and so on) offered in Word. See Chapter 3 for details. Here are some formats that are specific to Excel.

AutoFormat
To use **AutoFormat**:

1. Select the table. Click on **Format, AutoFormat** (Figure 5.15).

2. Select the desired format.

3. If you wish to modify one of the default format attributes, tick the relevant check box in the **Options** box, then carry out your changes and click on **OK**. Again, click on **OK** to confirm the format you have selected.

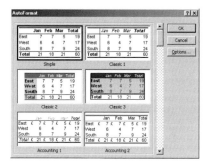

Figure 5.15 Choose AutoFormat.

Conditional formatting

Conditional formatting allows you to apply a format according to specific criteria. For example, you may wish the cell containing the profit to be displayed in a different colour if it is a negative amount, allowing you to spot immediately the size of the trouble.

To apply **conditional formatting**:

1. Select the relevant cell. Click on **Format, Conditional Formatting**.
2. In the second option of the **Condition 1** box, select the parameter to be applied.
3. In the third option of the **Condition 1** box, type the value. Click on the **Format** button.
4. In the **Color** option, select the colour to be used, then click on **OK** (Figure 5.16). Click on **OK** again.

Figure 5.16 The Conditional Formatting dialog box allows you to define a conditional format for certain cells.

Advanced Excel functions

Formulas

Functions

Scenarios

Sorting and filtering data

Auditing

Creating a chart

In this chapter we will use advanced Excel functions, such as creating formulas, using functions, sorting data, and so on.

Formulas

A formula allows simple arithmetical operations, such as addition or subtraction, to be carried out using the data in the worksheet.

Before you start, get to know the various mathematical operators used and their order of priority in terms of their application:

1. operations in brackets;
2. raising numbers to n power;
3. multiplication and division;
4. addition and subtraction.

Remember this order of priority and always bear it in mind when creating calculation formulas, otherwise you could end up with the wrong results.

Creating formulas

To create a formula:

- The formula is inserted into the cell that will contain the results.
- A formula always starts with the equals sign (=).
- A formula uses the reference of each cell included in the calculation. For example: =A1–B5.
- A formula may use numbers. For example: =4*5.

■ A formula uses one or all of the following symbols: + to add, – to subtract, * to multiply, / to divide, and an exponent to indicate an n power.

To create a formula with numbers:

1. Select the cell that will display the results of the formula. Press the = key, then type the formula.

2. Press **Enter** to confirm the formula or click on the green box in the Formula bar. Excel calculates the result and displays it in the originally selected cell.

To enter a formula with cell references:

1. Select the cell that will display the results of the formula. Press the = key.

2. Click on the first reference cell for the formula and press the arithmetical operator. Click on the second reference cell, and so on. Repeat this procedure for each cell in the formula.

3. When you have finished, press **Enter** to confirm the formula (Figure 6.1) or click on the green box in the Formula bar.

With the created formulas, Excel executes calculations and enters the outcome in the appropriate cells.

*Automatic calculation, in the context of formula creation, slows down the processing of the worksheet. If you wish to deactivate it, click on **Tools, Options**, then on the **Calculation** tab and finally on the **Manual** option (Figure 6.2). Confirm with **OK**.*

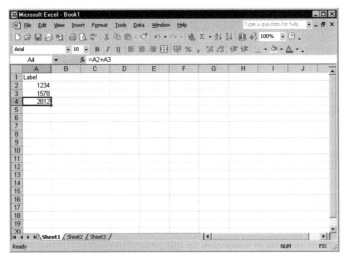

Figure 6.1 A formula in Excel.

Copying and moving formulas

When you copy a formula from one point in the worksheet to another, Excel adjusts the references to the new position. For example, when you copy cell C11, which contains the formula =SUM(C4:C10), and you insert it in D11, this displays =SUM(D4:D10). If you do not want Excel to adapt references and want instead to keep the initial cell references, you must give the instruction

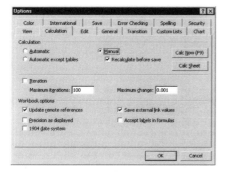

Figure 6.2 You can deactivate automatic calculation.

that the referenced cells are fixed and should not be modified. You must therefore mark up each reference cell as an absolute reference. Press **F4** immediately after having typed the reference. A dollar icon is displayed in front of the letter and number of the reference (for example D11).

Functions

Excel offers a number of predefined functions. They are available to carry out a series of operations on several values or on a range of values. For example, to calculate the average quarterly turnover, you can use the @AVERAGE function (A6:D6).

If you do not wish to use the F4 function key, type the $ sign in front of each reference letter or number.

There are three types of arguments: database, criteria and field arguments. The first two refer to cell ranges and the last to a column label.

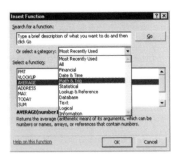

Figure 6.3 Use the Insert Function wizard to create your functions quickly.

Each function contains three distinct items:

- The @ sign marks the beginning of a formula. Therefore, if you type the = sign, Excel will replace it automatically with @.

- The name of the function, AVERAGE in our example, indicates the type of operation to be carried out.

- The argument, A6:D6 in our example, indicates the reference cells on whose values the function must operate. The argument is often a cell range. This could be an interest rate, a sorting order, and so on.

Wizard function

To make the task of entering functions and arguments easier, the wizard function will assist you.

To use the wizard function:

1. Click on the cell in which you want to insert the function. Click on **Insert, Function**.

2. Select the function category of your choice in the function category list. Select a function in the function name list. A description of the function selected is displayed in the lower part of the box (Figure 6.4). Click on **OK** to confirm your function. A dialog box is displayed for the selected function.

3. Work through the options, bearing in mind the instructions displayed in the lower part of the box. Click on **OK** or press the **Enter** key. Excel inserts the function as well as its argument in the selected cell and displays the results.

Figure 6.4 Defining the arguments (the data to be analysed) for a function.

When you use the **AutoSum** function, the cell range you wish to add must not contain blank cells.

Automatic entry

When processing a worksheet, the most frequently used function is working out a total.

To obtain the total of a row or a column, click on the cell at the edge of the row or the column. Click on the **AutoSum** button. In the cell, the range of the column or the row is displayed. Press **Enter** or click on the green box to confirm (Figure 6.5).

Scenarios

Scenarios allow you to create calculations based on theoretical values and to determine their effects on the results. Let us take a simple example: you are a writer and you wish to work out your potential royalties if you sell 500, 5000 or 10 000 copies of your book.

You can create a scenario with a few clicks:

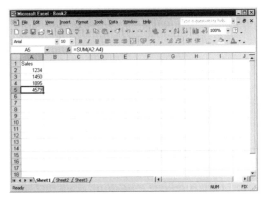

Figure 6.5 Clicking the Sum button allows you to add the contents of a column or row.

1. In your worksheet, click on **Tools, Scenarios**. The Scenarios manager is displayed and indicates that the worksheet does not contain a scenario. Click on the **Add** button.

2. Name the scenario in the appropriate area. Click on the **Changing cells** option (Figure 6.6).

3. In the worksheet, click on the cell in front of the one that will contain the scenario (in our example, the cell that contains the total sales). If you wish to modify several cells for the scenario, select each one by separating them with a semi-colon. Click on **OK** to confirm your cells. The **Scenario Values** dialog box displays the values shown in the cells to be edited.

4. Type the values to be used for the scenario, then click on **OK**. For our example, you should enter 500 and 5000. The Scenarios Manager displays the name of the scenario you have just created.

5. To display the results of a scenario, click on its name, then on the **Show** button.

Figure 6.6 The Add Scenario dialog box allows you to specify the cell you want to create the scenario in.

Sorting and filtering data

Once you have finished inserting functions and formulas, you can use some Excel tools that allow you to manage, sort and filter data.

Sorting data

When you type data, it is rare that you follow specific criteria. You must therefore sort your data as follows.

1. Select the cells range you wish to sort. Click on **Data, Sort** (Figure 6.7). Select the sort criterion in the **Sort by** box.

Figure 6.7 You can specify how you want your data sorted in the Sort dialog box.

*To sort a column quickly, you can use the **Ascending** or **Descending** buttons in the Standard toolbar.*

2. If required, select a second sorting criterion in the **Then by** box. Click on the option corresponding to your choice for each criterion (**Ascending** or **Descending**).

3. Specify whether the table contains a header in the **Header row** box. Click on **OK**.

Filtering data

When the worksheet contains several rows or columns, you can view only those on the screen. To access specific data, you can use the **Find** function (Chapter 1): the **Filtering** function allows access to any data within a few seconds.

To create automatic filtering:

1. Click on one of the cells, then on **Data, Filter, AutoFilter**. Each column header displays an arrow (Figure 6.8).

2. To implement a sort, click on the arrow in one of the headers, then select the filtering criteria to be used. Excel displays row numbers and the arrows of the headers of filtered data in blue.

Figure 6.8 By clicking on the arrow in one of the headers, you can select the filtering criteria to be used.

To customise the filter:

1. Click on the arrow of the header for which you wish to customise sorting, then select **Custom**.

2. Define the first filtering criterion in the area with the name of the column, then specify the second filtering criterion, if you need to, after having ticked the appropriate option (**And, Or**). Type the cell, the date, the town, the client, and so on, then click on **OK** (Figure 6.9).

*To delete a filter, click on the arrow in the relevant header, then on **All**.*

Auditing

Excel offers several auditing tools that allow you to check dependencies between cells. Once you have used the various auditing buttons, it is guaranteed that the results are correct.

*To deactivate AutoFilter, click on **Data, Filter, AutoFilter**.*

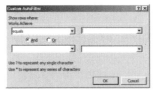

Figure 6.9 You can also create custom filters.

To implement an audit:

1. Click on **Tools, Auditing** (Figure 6.10).
2. Select the type of auditing to implement.

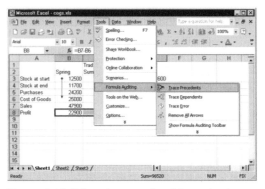

Figure 6.10 Select the type of auditing to implement.

To implement the various checks, click on the cell whose interdependencies you wish to check, then click on the button corresponding to the verification you wish to carry out in the Auditing toolbar.

Creating a chart

To simplify the task of creating a chart, Excel puts a wizard at your disposal.

To start the Chart Wizard:

1. Select the data you wish to use for your chart, then click on the **Chart Wizard** button.

    (a) **Chart type**. Lists the various charts that you can implement.

    (b) **Chart sub-type**. Displays the sub-types available for the type of chart selected. The description of the selected sub-type is displayed underneath this list.

2. Click on the type of chart to be applied. Click on the chart sub-type. The **Press and Hold to View Sample** button allows you, by clicking on it and keeping it pressed, to view the chart you are creating (Figure 6.11). Click on the **Next** button.

    (a) **Data Range**. Allows you to modify the range previously selected and to specify the position of the data (Figure 6.12).

    (b) **Series**. Allows you to edit, add or delete a series.

3. When you have finished your modifications, click on the **Next** button. This step allows you to create settings for one or more items in the chart. The

Figure 6.11 Select the type and sub-type of the chart you want.

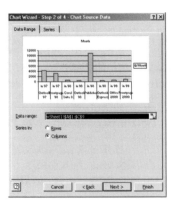

Figure 6.12 The second step of the Chart Wizard is to select the source data.

dialog box has several buttons you can use for your editing: Titles, Data Table, Axes, Legend, Data Labels and Gridlines (Figure 6.13).

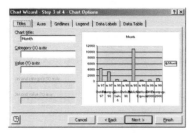

Figure 6.13 The third step of the Chart Wizard is to chose the options you want for Titles, Data Tables, Axes, Legend, Data Labels and Gridlines.

4. When you have chosen your options, click on the **Next** button. This final step allows you to specify the address for the chart (Figure 6.14).

(a) **As new sheet**. Allows you to add a worksheet chart to your workbook. If you choose this option, remember to enter the name of the new worksheet.

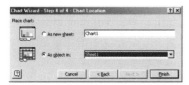

Figure 6.14 The fourth and final step of the Chart Wizard is to choose the location of the chart.

(b) **As object in**. Allows you to insert the chart in the worksheet where you have selected the data. This is an embedded, but independent object. You can easily move or resize it because it is not linked to the cells in the worksheets.

5. Once you have defined these options, click on the **Finish** button.

According to the options in the fourth step, the chart is inserted into a chart worksheet or into the active worksheet.

To select a chart, click on it. Around the chart, Excel displays small squares known as 'handles'.

To move the chart, click on the chart. Then, keeping the button pressed, drag it to where you want to place it and release the mouse button.

To reduce or enlarge a chart, click on one of the handles, then drag to achieve the size you want.

Editing a chart

Excel offers several options for controlling the appearance and functioning of a chart. There are several tools available for editing charts:

- **Chart menu**. Available when the chart is selected. Offers options that allow you to edit the type, to select other data, to add data and so on.
- **Context menu**. Available with a click of the right mouse button on any object in the chart.
- **Chart toolbar**. Allows you to edit format, objects, type, legend, to display the data table, and so on (Table 6.1).

Table 6.1 Buttons in the Chart toolbar

Button	Action
Chart Area ▾	Displays the list of the items in the chart. By clicking on the item of your choice in this list, you select it.
	Opens a dialog box that lets you apply formats to the selected item.
	Chooses another type of chart.
	Displays or hides a legend.
	Activates or deactivates the data table which displays the data in the chart.
	Shows the data selected by row.
	Shows the data selected by column.
	Angles text downward, from left to right.
	Angles text upward, from left to right.

Basic PowerPoint functions

7

In this chapter, we will study the basic functions of PowerPoint, such as opening a new presentation, formatting and so on.

The first step

When you start the program, the New Presentation display is in the Task Pane (Figure 7.1). From this dialog box, you can choose a number of options:

Figure 7.1   The New Presentation display allows you to choose how you will create a new presentation.

- **Open an existing presentation**. Allows you to display a previously created presentation.
- **New**. Allows you to open a blank presentation or to start from a Design Template or wizard. You can also start a new presentation based on an existing one.

- **New from Template**. Allows you to select themes, backgrounds, predefined presentations, animation and so on.

Converting a presentation

You can also open a presentation created in another program. Click on the **Open** button in the Standard toolbar. In the **Files of type** box, select the application in which the required document was created. Double-click on it in the list that is displayed. PowerPoint automatically converts the presentation so that it can be modified.

Applying a template

You can change a format by changing it to a predefined template. To apply a template to an already created presentation:

1. Click on **Format, Slide Design** (Figure 7.2).
2. Click on a design to apply it to all the slides, or click the arrow bar and select **Apply to Selected Slides**.

AutoContent Wizard

When you require a presentation quickly, use the AutoContent Wizard:

1. Click on **AutoContent Wizard** in the New Presentation Task Pane. If this is not active, click on **File, New**. Click on the **General** tab. Double-click on the **AutoContent Wizard** icon. Click on **Next**.
2. Now choose the presentation type (Figure 7.3). PowerPoint offers a number of themes to cater for most business needs. Press a category button (list on the left) for the type of presentation you are going to give and then select the presentation that best fits your needs (list on the right). You can add one of your own presentations by choosing a category and then pressing **Add**. Click on **Next**.

*If the PowerPoint dialog box is not displayed, click on **Tools, Options**. Click on the **View** tab. Tick the **Startup** dialog option, then click on **OK** to confirm.*

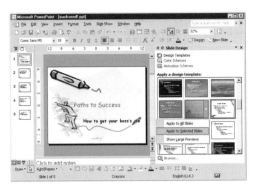

Figure 7.2 You can apply a template to a presentation that has already been created.

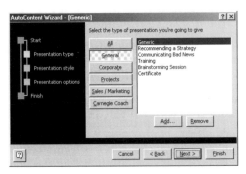

Figure 7.3 Choosing the presentation type.

3. You must now select the type of output for your presentation. Click on **Next**.

4. You can specify the presentation title, the contents of the footer, the slide number and so on. Click on **Next**, then on **Finish**.

Display views

PowerPoint offers several ways for viewing a presentation. Each view allows a different type of intervention:

■ **Normal**. This gives you a three-sided view: on the left, an Outline pane, in the centre, a Slide pane, and at the bottom, a Notes pane. This allows you to work on the presentation structure, contents and notes all at the same time (Figure 7.4). This is the default display view.

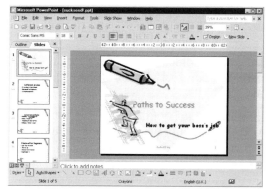

Figure 7.4 Slide view in Normal viewing mode.

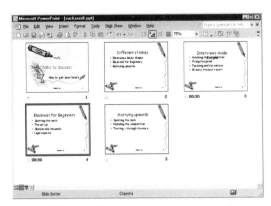

Figure 7.5 Slide Sorter view gives you a good overview of your show.

- **Slide Sorter view**. Allows you to view all the slides in your presentation. This is the ideal view to sort, move and copy slides.
- **Slide Show**. Allows you to view the set of slides in sequence. In this view, the slide takes up the whole screen. You can test the actual show and any animation effects you have created.

To change the view, click on the appropriate display button in the bottom left corner of the window (Figure 7.6). You can also click on **View**, then make your choice.

Figure 7.6 Viewing mode buttons.

If you wish to enlarge or reduce any part of a slide, click on **View, Zoom**. Choose the zoom percentage (Figure 7.7).

Figure 7.7 You can use the Zoom dialog box to change the view on screen.

New presentations

Let us now see how to create a new presentation.

1. Click on **Blank presentation** in the New Presentation Task Pane display, or on **File, New**.
2. In the Slide Layout display in the Task Pane, choose the type of slide to be created by clicking on the relevant icon (Figure 7.8). The right-hand side of the box displays a textual description of the selected type. Click on **OK**. The number of the slide is displayed in the status bar (slide x of y).

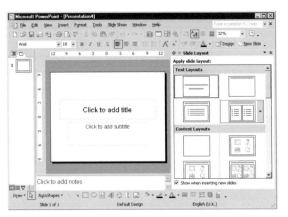

Figure 7.8 You can choose between AutoLayouts in the Slide Layout display.

Inserting, deleting and formatting slides

■ To delete a slide, display it in Outline or Slide Sorter view, then click on it and press the delete key.

■ New Slide Insert slides by clicking on the **New Slide** button. Select the type of slide as explained above and click on **OK**. PowerPoint inserts the new slide and assigns the previous format to it.

You can also click on **Insert, New Slide**, or select a slide in the Outline bar and press the Enter Key. Repeat the above procedures to choose the type of slide.

- If you are not happy with your choice of slide, you can change it. Click on the **format** menu and select **Slide Layout** (Figure 7.9). Select the new type.

Figure 7.9 You can change the layout of your slide in the Slide Layout display.

Moving between slides

- To navigate between slides in Normal view, click on the up or down double arrow in the vertical scroll bar. You can also drag the scroll bar. A balloon displays the number of pages while you are scrolling. Release when you get to the slide you wish to display.

- To navigate between slides in Slide Sorter view, click on the slide to be selected (Figure 7.10).

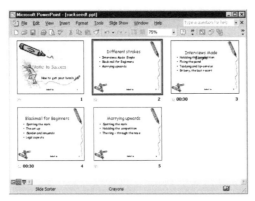

Figure 7.10 Move quickly between slides in the Slide Sorter.

Text

Once you have selected the type of slide you wish to create, you can start inserting text. Whatever the type of slide you have chosen, you follow the same procedures:

The text automatically fits the frame.

■ To insert text, click on one of the text boxes that reads **Click to add**. The frame around the text box becomes greyed and the pointer flashes. Type your text. To exit from the text box, click outside it. You can write whatever you want as you would do in a text processing program; the line feed is automatic.

To activate Auto-fit text:

1. Click on **Tools, Auto Correct Options**, then on the Autoformat As You Type tab (Figure 7.11).

Figure 7.11 Activating the Auto-fit text.

2. Tick the **Auto-fit text to text placeholder** option to activate it. Click on **OK**.

Selecting text
For any editing or deleting operation, you must know how to select the text on which to act. These procedures are explained later in this book.

Bulleted lists
A bulleted list presentation is extremely practical because it allows each topic to be displayed point by point. To display a slide of this type, click on the **Bulleted list** template in the Slide Layout display.

The function that allows the text to fit automatically to the text frame is not active for titles.

*To insert a text box, click on the **Text Box** button in the Drawing toolbar and draw the frame in the slide.*

*To change a bulleted list to normal text, select the list, then click on the **Bullets** button to deactivate it.*

The 'bullet' is the icon displayed to the left of each topic. Type the text in the area that contains the bulleted list, then press the **Enter** key each time you wish to display a new bullet. By default, PowerPoint displays small round black bullets.

To create a bulleted list, you can also select a text, then click on the **Bullets** button in the Formatting toolbar.

You can change the type of bullets used:

1. In the bulleted list, press **Ctrl+A** to select the entire list.
2. Click with the right mouse button on the selection, then select **Bullets and Numbering** (Figure 7.12). Click on the type of bullet you want. You can modify the colour and size of the bullets in the **Color** and **Size** options. The customize button allows you to select a letter or any other icon as a bullet. Click on **OK**.

Figure 7.12 Selecting a different bullet style in the Bullets and Numbering dialog box.

PowerPoint also allows you to use a ClipArt picture as a bullet. In the **Bullets and Numbering** dialog box, click on the **Bulleted** tab, then on the **Picture** button. In the Picture Bullet dialog box, click on the bullet of your choice, then on OK.

Harmonisation

PowerPoint allows you to harmonise presentations thanks to its masters and colour schemes.

Slide Master

The Slide Master controls font, size of characters for all titles, bullet lists, sub-titles and so on, and contains the charts shared by all the slides. It also allows you to insert date, slide number and any other information you may wish to include.

To display the Slide Master for a slide, click on **View, Master**. In the drop-down menu, select **Slide Maste**r. Then follow the instructions below to use or edit the Slide Master:

- To edit titles, select the master title, then use the **Font** and **Size** drop-down list. For more complex modifications, use the Font dialog box; to open it, click on **Format, Font**.
- To edit the text in bulleted lists, select the bulleted list in the master, then use the **Font** and **Size** drop-down list. You can use other buttons in the Formatting toolbar such as the **Font Size** arrow.

Slide Master controls all aspects of slides. When you edit an area in the master, the modifications apply to all the slides in the presentation. If you do not wish to use this format for all of the slides, display the slide to be unformatted in Slide view, then click on **Format, Background**. In the dialog box, tick the **Omit background graphics from master** option to activate it, then click on **Apply**.

Colour schemes

Each predefined template offers a different colour for each of the items in slides: titles, bulleted lists, numbered lists, fill and so on. You can easily modify the colour for each category of items as follows:

1. Click on format, Slide Design to display Slide Design in the Task Pane, then click on colour schemes (Figure 7.13).

2. In the Task Pane, you can choose a standard scheme or customise your own scheme. It is better, however, to use a standard scheme to avoid problems (clashing colours and so on). If you do not like any of the standard schemes, click on Edit Colour Schemes, then select a colour for each element of the slides. Once you have completed your choice open the menu from the arrow bar on the preview and click on **Apply to All** so that the colour scheme applies to the whole presentation or click on **Apply** so that it applies only to the selected slide.

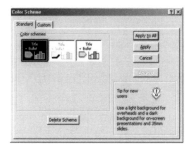

Figure 7.13 Colour schemes allow you to harmonise your presentation.

Formatting slides

Just as in Word, you can create a custom format.

Tips for formatting text
To format text, you must first select it as explained earlier in this chapter. To select all the text in a slide in Outline view, click on its icon. In Slide view, simply press **Ctrl+A**.

For text, formatting options are the same as in Word (see Chapter 3). Here we provide some hints and tips:

- **Slide Master view**. Allows you to modify the appearance of text for all slides. To give coherence to the format, carry out the modifications in the master.

- **Slide view**. Displays the various slides of the presentation one by one. To format the text of one slide differently from the master, use this view because it allows you to see the text exactly as it will appear in the slide show.

Background
Each slide has a background, which may or may not be coloured depending on how you created the slide.

If you have added text boxes to some slides, the master cannot control them.

Figure 7.14 Choosing a background colour.

To modify the background:

1. Click on **Format, Background** (Figure 7.14).
2. To choose a background colour, click on the arrow in the **Background fill** drop-down list, then choose the colour. To choose another colour, click on the **More Colors** button, then choose a colour or specify it yourself. The **Fill Effects** options allow you to select a gradient, texture, pattern or picture for the background. Click on **OK**.

Pictures

Pictures are great to use in a slide show because they support the presentation and explain visually – and therefore more immediately – the contents of the slides.

PowerPoint allows you to insert several types of pictures:

- Digital pictures, produced with a scanner or a digital camera.
- Vector pictures produced with image-creation programs, such as Illustrator. These are created from mathematical shapes and are made up of basic elements: lines, regular areas and so on.

■ Pictures from the Office Clip Organizer.

Remember that a digital picture may be in black and white, greyscale or colour.

To insert a picture, follow the procedures given in Chapter 2.

Picture toolbar

The Picture toolbar allows you to retouch a picture. This is displayed automatically when you select a picture (by clicking on it) and offers buttons for editing contrast, brightness, cropping, display in colour or black and white, and so on. Refer to Table 7.1 to see how to use these buttons.

Table 7.1 The buttons in the Picture toolbar

Button	Action
	Insert Picture from File. Inserts an existing picture in the active file at the insertion point.
	Image Control. Changes a picture colour to greyscale, black and white or as a watermark (a transparent image that appears under the text without hiding it).
	More Contrast. Increases the picture contrast.
	Less Contrast. Decreases the picture contrast.

Button	Action
☼↑	**More Brightness**. Increases the picture brightness.
☼↓	**Less Brightness**. Decreases the picture brightness.
⊬	**Crop**. Trims or restores portions of a picture. Click on this icon, then drag a sizing handle on the picture.
	Rotate left. Rotate the image 90° anti-clockwise.
≡	**Line Style**. Modifies the lines framing the picture.
	Compress Pictures. Reduces the file size of images by discarding any cropped areas, and/or by reducing the resolution.
	Recolor Picture. To enable this command, select a single picture or OLE object.
	Format Object. Defines formatting options for the picture.
	Set Transparent Color. Makes one of the colours in the picture transparent.
	Reset Picture. Restores the picture to its original status.

Charts

When giving presentations, you often need to present series of figures. In such a situation, the audience does not have a great deal of time to understand and analyse figures. To help overcome this problem, add a chart to simplify the figures and to make your point clearly and forcefully.

 If you have created your slides with AutoContent Wizard or you have selected a slide predefined for charts, simply double-click on the **Double-click to add chart** message. If you have chosen a blank slide, or if you wish to insert a chart in a text slide, you must click on the **Insert, Chart** button in the Standard toolbar.

Whichever procedure you use, the PresentationNumber – Datasheet window is displayed with data as examples.

To enter the data you wish to format, click on the cell you want, type the data, then press **Enter** to confirm. You must use the direction keys to move within the table cells. By default, data are arranged by rows. Column titles are displayed on the horizontal axis (x) in the chart. If you want to arrange your data by columns, with row titles on the x axis, click on the **By Column** button in the Standard toolbar.

Refer to Chapter 6 for further information on creating and modifying charts.

OLE is a special interprogram technology that allows you to share information between programs. All Office programs support the OLE technology.

Advanced PowerPoint functions

8

In this chapter, we will examine advanced PowerPoint functions, such as drawing, placing objects, organising a slide show and so on.

Placing objects

You have several methods available for placing your items exactly.

Ruler and guides

To place an object exactly, the ruler and the guides are indispensable.

To activate the ruler, click on **View, Ruler**. When you drag the object, a dotted line will appear in the ruler, showing the exact position of the object edge. Release when you are exactly where you want to be (Figure 8.1).

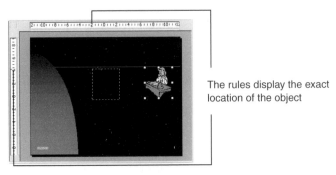

The rules display the exact location of the object

Figure 8.1 You can place objects exactly with the ruler.

To activate the guides, click on **View, Grid and Guides**. On the screen you will see a dotted cross. When you drag an object on to a guide, the object sticks to it. To move a guide, click on it, then drag it to where you want to be. This allows you to align objects on the slide with absolute perfection (Figure 8.2).

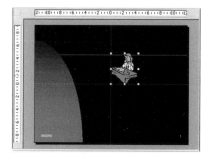

Figure 8.2 The guides help you to position two objects exactly.

Arranging objects

While you are creating your slide, you pile up objects until you can no longer see the objects in the background. If you wish to modify one of the hidden objects, you must bring it back to the foreground. If the object is still visible, click on it; otherwise, click with the right mouse button on one of the objects of the pile, then select **Order**. In the sub-menu (Figure 8.3), click on the choice you want:

- **Bring to Front**. Places the selected object on top of the pile.
- **Send to Back**. Places the selected object at the bottom of the pile.

■ **Bring Forward**. Brings the selected object forward by one place.

■ **Send Backward**. Sends the selected object backward by one place.

Figure 8.3 The options available for organising your objects.

Drawing

With PowerPoint, you can insert shapes and arrows and draw and create tables for your presentations.

Drawing toolbar

The various drawing tools are available in the Drawing toolbar at the bottom of the screen. You can draw lines, shapes and arrows, or even select AutoShapes. Simply click on the tool, then insert it into the slide. Use the various buttons to add colour, modify the line style and so on.

Creating tables

To create a table for a presentation, click on **Insert, Table** (Figure 8.4). Define the number of columns and rows for the table, then click on **OK**.

Figure 8.4 Inserting a table into a presentation.

To insert new rows or columns, use the pointer, which has now become a pencil, and draw.

The procedures to move between cells, insert text, modify the colour and so on are identical to those used for tables in Word (see Chapter 4).

Style coherence

PowerPoint offers a tool for checking the style of the presentation and its coherence. To activate the checking of the style:

1. Click on **Tools, Options**, then on the **Spelling and Style** tab.

2. In the Style area, tick the **Check style** option box (Figure 8.5). Click on **OK**. Note that you must enable the Office Assistant for this to work.

Figure 8.5 Activating the style checker.

To define the style to be used:

1. In the **Spelling and Style** tab, click on the **Style Options** button (Figure 8.6). The two tabs, **Case and End Punctuation** and **Visual Clarity**, give you all the options you need for your checks.

2. Specify the options required, the title text size, the title case, the sentence case and so on. Click on **OK** to confirm.

If your presentation has any style discrepancies, PowerPoint warns you with a dialog box.

Figure 8.6 Setting the style options to achieve the desired style coherence.

Sorting, structuring and adapting slides

To make your slide show perfect, you must sort the slides. The best way to do this is by using the Slide Sorter view. Click on the **Slide Sorter View** button at the bottom left of the screen (Figure 8.7).

To copy a slide:

1. Click on the slide and press the **Ctrl** key.
2. Keeping this key pressed, drag the slides. A vertical line follows the drag, showing you where the copy is going to be inserted when you release the key.

To move a slide, repeat the above procedure without pressing the **Ctrl** key.

To delete a slide, click on it, then press the **delete** key.

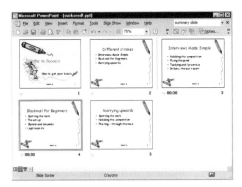

Figure 8.7 Slide Sorter.

To move slides, you can also use the Outline view. In this view, all slides are reduced to their title levels. You can then move them by dragging their icons up or down. A horizontal line moves as you move, showing where the slide will be placed when you release the mouse button. You can also move the slide with the **Up** or **Down** buttons in the Outlining toolbar.

Organising a slide show with the summary slide

When you create a slide show to be shown on a computer or on the Web, you can use a summary slide as a starting point, which contains a bulleted list with the titles of all the slides in the presentation. When you start the slide show, you can choose the direction you wish to follow from the summary slide.

To create a summary slide:

1. In Slide Sorter view, click on the first slide to be included in the summary slide.

2. Press the **Ctrl** key, then click on the second slide, and so on, keeping the key pressed.

3. Click on the **Summary Slide** button in the Slide Sorter view or Outlining toolbar (Figure 8.8).

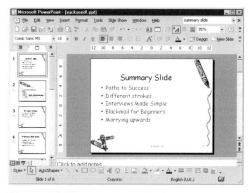

Figure 8.8 The summary slide allows you to see the structure of the presentation.

Creating bookmarks

 To navigate more quickly through the presentation, you can create bookmarks that allow direct access to the required place when you click on them.

To create a bookmark:

1. In the slide, select the relevant text.

2. Click on the **Insert Hyperlink** button (Figure 8.9).

Refer to Chapter 1 to discover the new PowerPoint Web functions. These allow you to create a frame sequence at the left of the window, so Web surfers can access the slides of interest by clicking on that frame.

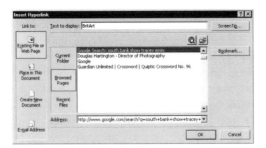

Figure 8.9 Inserting a hyperlink with the Insert Hyperlink dialog box.

3. Click on the **Bookmark** button (Figure 8.10). Click on the name of the slide you want. Click on **OK** in the two dialog boxes.

Narration
PowerPoint allows you to add a sound commentary to your slide show. Before recording your narration, look at the various buttons and what they do:

■ To pause during the slide show, right-click anywhere in the active slide, then click on **Pause Narration**.

Figure 8.10 Creating bookmarks in a slide.

■ To start recording again, click with the right button, then click on **Resume Narration**.

To record a narration:

1. Switch on your computer and check the connection. Click on **Slide Show, Record Narration** (Figure 8.11). Click **OK**.

2. Click on the next slide to move it without interrupting the commentary.

   At the end of the slide show, a message is displayed asking if you wish to save the slide timings as well as the narrations that have been saved for each slide.

3. To accept, click on **Yes**. To save only the commentary without timings, click on **No**.

Figure 8.11 Starting the Record Narration function.

When you scroll through the slide show, the commentary is started automatically so that the audience can follow your presentation better.

If you do not want the commentary to start with the slide show:

1. Click on **Slide Sorter view**.

2. Right-click on one of the images and select **Set Up Show** (Figure 8.12).

Figure 8.12 Deactivating the Record Narration function.

3. Click on **Show without narration**, then on **OK**.

Adapting the slide show to the audience

PowerPoint allows you to adapt the slide show according to your audience, for example, excluding some information from certain audiences. To control a slide show:

1. Click on **Slide Show, Custom Shows**. Click on the **New** button.

2. In the **Define Custom Show** dialog box (Figure 8.13), name the slide show in the **Slide show name** option. In the list on the left, click on the first slide to be inserted, then click on the **Add** button. Repeat this procedure for each slide you wish to insert. To put your slides in a different order, click on the name of the relevant slide in the right-hand window, then click on the up or down arrow buttons.

Figure 8.13 Customising your slide show to suit your audience.

3. Click on **OK** to save the custom slide show.

To launch the controlled slide show, click on **Slide Show, Custom Show**. Select the show you want, then click on the **Show** button to start it.

Animation

We will now look at creating animation effects.

Animating transitions between slides

In a standard slide show, the speaker must press a button or click on an icon to move to the next slide. This technique can be inefficient because there is usually a lack of synchronisation between the speaker's voice and what you see on screen. With PowerPoint, you can time transitions between each slide and create animations.

To manage transitions between slides:

1. Click on the slide to be animated, then on the Slide **Transition** item in the **Slide Show** menu.

2. Select a transition effect from the list at the top of the Task Pane. The display area shows the effect of the selected transition.

3. Click on the required option in the speed drop-down list (**Slow**, **Medium** or **Fast**) to define the speed of the transition. In the **Advance** area, click on **On mouse click** to control the slides' progression manually, or click on **Automatically after** for PowerPoint to automatically display the following slide after the specified number of seconds.

4. To assign sound to the transition, click on the arrow in the **Sound** drop-down list, then select the sound you want. For the sound to last until the next slide comes on, click on **Loop until next sound**. The settings are automatically applied to the selected slide. If you click on **Apply to All**, the specified effects will apply to all the slides.

Animating slides

You can also animate images, text, bulleted lists, and so on in the slides. These animations are available from the Animation Preview icon in the Animation Effects toolbar displayed in Slide Show:

1. Display the relevant slide with the Slide Show view, then select **Animation Schemes** from the **Slide Show** menu.

2. Select the effect you want from the drop-down list. It will be automatically applied to the current slide. Click **Apply to All Slides** if you want to use the same effect on them all. (Figure 8.14)

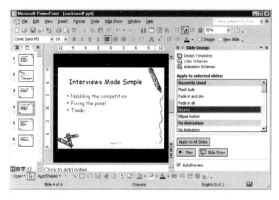

Figure 8.14 Applying an animation scheme. When you click on a scheme name, it will be previewed in the slide display.

Customising animation effects

PowerPoint allows you to create more targeted animation effects:

1. Click on **Slide Show, Custom Animation** (Figure 8.15).

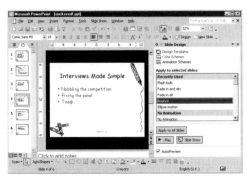

Figure 8.15 Customising the animation of a slide show.

2. Select an object on the slide. Click the **Add Effects** button (or **Change** if an animation scheme has been applied), then in turn set the options for the object's **Entrance**, **Emphasis**, **Exit** and **Motion Paths**. As you set each option, you can modify its speed, direction, size, font or other aspect, as applicable, in the **Modify** area of the Task Pane. The effect will be previewed after each change.

You can add as many effects as you like to a single object, but do keep your audience in mind!

Starting a slide show

Let us now see what the slide show is like and check that it works.

To start the slide show, display the first slide, then click on the **Slide Show** button at the bottom of the screen. You can also click on **View, Slide Show**. The slide is displayed on the whole of the screen. To scroll the slide show, follow the procedures shown below:

- To scroll the slide show slide after slide, click anywhere in the screen or press the arrow keys at the bottom of your keyboard.
- The slide show scrolls automatically if you have defined a specific transition time.
- Press the **Esc** key to exit from the slide show.
- To display the slide show control menu, right-click on the greyed button in the bottom left corner of the slide.
- Double-click on the audio or video clips icon to open them.

Slide shows on paper, slides or other media

So far, we have seen a slide show only on screen. However, you can transfer slides on to transparencies, 35 mm slides or paper.

To specify the medium for your presentation, click on **File, Page Setup** (Figure 8.16). To adapt your slides to the medium you are going to use, click on the arrow in the **Slides sized for** drop-down list and select the option corresponding to your medium:

- **Letter Paper**. 8.5" × 11" format.
- **A4 Paper**. Corresponds to the traditional 210 × 297 mm size.
- **35 mm Slides**. Corresponds to the photo slides format.
- **Overhead**. For overhead projectors.
- **Banner**. For printing on continuous paper.
- **Custom**. Allows you to fit the size of your slides to the printer's print area.

You can also change the orientation of your slides (Landscape or Portrait).

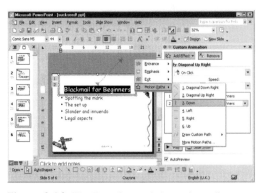

Figure 8.16 The Page Setup dialogue box allows you to specify the medium you are going to use for your slide show.

Inserted notes are not visible to the audience.

Speaker notes

To avoid memory lapses during your slide show, you may want to create some notes. These notes can be entered in the bottom right area in the Normal view.

Transferring a slide show

You may need to transfer your slide show, for example if you are doing presentations at several locations. PowerPoint offers a wizard that helps you put the whole of your presentation on a disk.

To start this wizard:

1. Click on **File, Pack and Go**. The Pack and Go Wizard is displayed. Click on the **Next** button to display the second window for this wizard.

2. Select the presentation you wish to export. Click on the **Next** button to continue. Specify the type of computer you wish to use for your presentation. Click on the **Next** button.

3. You must now include linked files or include TrueType fonts in your presentation. Once you have finished your choice, click on the **Next** button. The wizard offers to load PowerPoint Viewer in case the computer on which you are planning to install your presentation does not run PowerPoint. Click on the **Next** button, then click on the **Finish** button.

   The wizard loads your data on to the disk in your floppy disk drive. Have several disks at the ready, just in case.

Basic Outlook functions

9

In this chapter, we will study the basic functions of Outlook, its main folders, what you can do with them, and so on.

Discovering Outlook

With Outlook, you can exchange e-mail, share information with other Office applications, and manage a variety of information concerning your activities (appointments, meetings, clients, tasks, and so on).

When you first start Outlook, you may need to configure the installation of Outlook as well as the Internet connection. Follow the steps indicated by the wizard.

Figure 9.1 The Outlook bar.

The Outlook bar

The Outlook bar, positioned to the left of the screen, allows you to navigate between the program folders (you will find a description of this later on). If this is not displayed, click on **View, Outlook bar**. To display the folder of your choice, click on its shortcut in the Outlook bar: it is displayed in the central window (Figure 9.1).

Underneath the Outlook bar there are two buttons that allow access to other group bars. To open one of these groups, click on the corresponding button.

- **My Shortcuts** offers folders that help manage, organise and sort your e-mail messages.
- **Other Shortcuts** offer quick access to folders or files in another application.

Outlook Today

This folder lists today's activities and allows access to Messages folders (Figure 9.2). It is a reminder of your activities and daily work.

Customising Outlook Today

By default, the Outlook Today folder displays all the tasks to be carried out as well as the contents of your Inbox dialog box. You can customise options for this folder and ask, for example, for it to be displayed automatically when you open the program.

To customise Outlook Today:

1. In the Outlook Today folder, click on the **Customize Outlook Today** option.
2. In the customisation options (Figure 9.3), specify your choices. When you have finished, click on **Save Changes**.

Figure 9.2 The Outlook Today folder.

Figure 9.3 You can customise the Outlook Today folder.

Calendar

This folder plans your activities. It allows you to manage your time, note your appointments, plan your meetings, establish a list of your daily tasks, and so on. To display it, click on **Calendar** in the Outlook bar. Calendar offers three main items: Appointments, Dates and TaskPad (Figure 9.4).

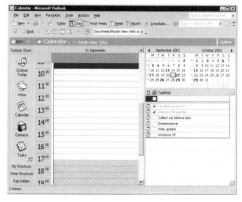

Figure 9.4 Outlook's Calendar folder.

Contacts

This is your address book. To display it, click on the **Contacts** icon in the Outlook bar (Figure 9.5).

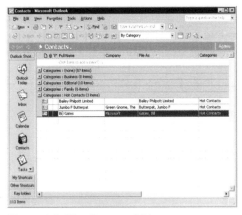

Figure 9.5 The Contacts folder.

The Contacts folder is your address book. It is available to all Office applications to send messages, make telephone calls, and so on.

If you have a modem, you can quickly dial a telephone number in this folder, send an e-mail message and even go to one of your correspondents' Web pages. To learn how to create or phone a contact, see Chapter 10.

Tasks

A task is a professional or personal mission you need to carry out to its completion (reports, investigations, and so on). The Tasks folder allows you to create various tasks, to follow their status, to assign them to another person, and so on. To display this folder, click on the **Tasks** icon in the Outlook bar (Figure 9.6).

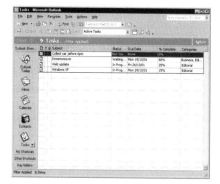

Figure 9.6 The Tasks folder.

Managing tasks

To create a task, click on the **Tasks** folder icon in the Outlook bar. Click on the **New** button in the Standard toolbar. If it is not already displayed, click on the **Task** tab (Figure 9.7). In the **Subject** box, type the subject or the definition of your task. In the **Due date** box, choose the date you wish to set as the deadline for your task, either by entering a date or by clicking on the appropriate date in the drop-down calendar. If you do not wish to set a deadline, click on the **None** check box. Give the start date in the **Start date** box. The **Status** option allows you to assign a holiday period during the implementation of the task. You can also indicate a priority level, a completion percentage, a reminder signal – with sound, if you want – defined by date and time, a category, and so on. Once you have defined your choices, click on the **Save and Close** button. The task you have created is displayed in the tasks list in the Tasks folder as well as in Calendar.

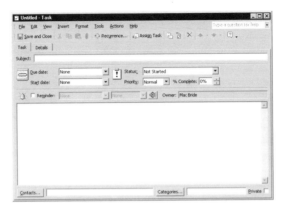

Figure 9.7 Creating a task.

When a task is completed, click on the check box in front of the completed task in the tasks list. A tick appears in the check box and Outlook crosses it out to indicate that it is complete. If you wish to delete it, select it, then click on the **Delete** button in the Standard toolbar.

Journal

This folder is your diary. You can record meetings with clients, and store items, messages, and so on. You can also create a journal entry without reference to an item. To display this folder, click on **Shortcuts** in the Outlook bar, then on **Journal** (Figure 9.8).

Figure 9.8 The Journal folder.

Creating journal entries

You can create two types of records or entries for your journal: automatic records and manual records.

To create a manual journal entry without links to any item:

1. Click on the **New** button in the Standard toolbar (Figure 9.9).

2. In the **Subject** box, type the wording for your entry. Click on the arrow of the **Entry type** option and select the type you want. In the **Company** box, type the name of the relevant company. In the **Start time** box, specify the required date. Click on the **Categories** button if you wish to indicate a category. Type your comments in the text box. Click on the **Save and Close** button when you have finished.

In the Journal folder, click on the **+** icon next to the entry type of your choice to display the list of entries of this type.

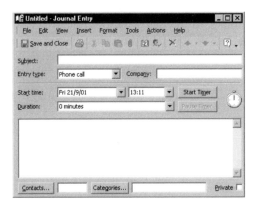

Figure 9.9 Creating a journal entry.

To delete automatic record-
ing of activities or contacts
*click **Tools, Options**, then*
***Journal Options**. Point to*
the entry to be deleted,
then click on the right
*button. Select **Delete** in the*
*context menu. Click on **OK***
to confirm your deletion.

To create a manual entry linked to an item:

1. Select the item (contact, task, message, and so on), click on **Tools, Save to journal**.

2. Carry out your modifications as required in the dialog box. Click on the **Save and Close** button.

To delete a journal entry, click on it in the list, then on the **Delete** button in the toolbar.

To create automatic journal entries:

1. In the Journal folder, click on **Tools, Options**.

Figure 9.10 A note.

2. In the dialog box, click on the **Journal Options** button. Tick the check boxes of the items you wish to record in the journal. Click on the contacts for which you wish to record elements. If you wish to record all the elements of an application, click on the check box in the **Also record files from** box. Click **OK**.

All the activities will scroll in the programs, and the contacts or the tasks that you have selected will be recorded in the Journal folder.

Notes

Outlook offers an electronic version of Post-it notes. Use Notes to jot down ideas or reminders.

To create a note, click on **Notes** in the Outlook bar. Click on the **New** button, then type the text of the note (Figure 9.10). When you have finished, click on the **Close** button.

To customise a note, click on the note icon in the top left corner of the Note window, point to **Color**, then choose a colour.

To open a note, double-click on it. It will be displayed on top of all the other Desktop windows. If you change to another window, the note will go into the background. To find the note again, simply click on its button in the taskbar.

Inbox

The Inbox allows you to organise your e-mail and display received messages (Figure 9.11). This is the folder that is displayed by default when you start Outlook. It shows the list of messages you have received. To read a message, double-click on it in the list. You can learn more about this folder in Chapter 10.

Creating contacts

In this folder, you can list all your contacts with their addresses, telephone numbers, e-mail addresses, and so on. You can use this record whenever you want to e-mail or telephone a contact.

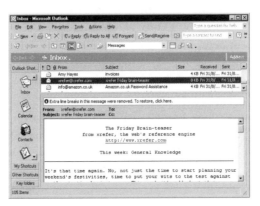

Figure 9.11 The Inbox displays your e-mail messages, both sent and received.

To create a business card, click on the **New** button in the toolbar (Figure 9.12). Click on the **Contact** button, type the title, name and surname of the relevant person, then click on **OK**. Type in all the other required options. Once you have finished, click on the **Save and New** button to save your business card and open a new blank card, or the **Save and Close** button if you do not wish to enter another business card.

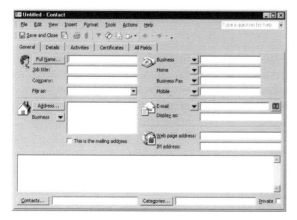

Figure 9.12 Creating a business card in the Contact dialog box.

Once you have entered your business cards, they will appear in the Contacts folder in alphabetical order. When you want to access one, click on the first letter of the contact name in the **Alphabet** tab.

To select a business card, click on it. To display all the information it contains, double-click on the card.

Making a telephone call from a business card

If you have a modem connected to your computer and your telephone line, and your telephone is connected to your modem, Outlook lets you make calls directly from your computer.

To make a telephone call, click on the business card of the person you wish to call, then click the **Dial** button in the Standard toolbar. Click on the number you wish to call. The **New Call** dialog box is displayed (Figure 9.13). Click on the **Start Call** button. Outlook dials the number and displays a dialog box that prompts you to lift the receiver. Click on the **Speak** button when you get through to your correspondent. Click on **End Call** when the conversation is over.

Sending e-mail messages

If your contact has an e-mail address, you can send a message from the Contacts folder.

To send an e-mail message, click on the person's business card, then on the **New Call** button in the Standard toolbar. A dialog box is displayed containing the address of the person you have selected. Type a title in the **Object** text box, type the complete message in the large message area positioned in the bottom part of the dialog box, then click on the **Send** button.

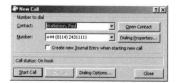

Figure 9.13 Making a telephone call through Outlook.

Advanced Outlook functions

Using Calendar

Sending and receiving e-mail messages

In this chapter, we will study the advanced functions of Outlook, such as creating appointments, organising meetings, sending messages, and so on.

Using Calendar

Outlook puts a calendar at your disposal to record your appointments, plan your meetings and organise your holidays. You can also use this function to remind you about meetings and appointments.

Before we look at the procedures you need to follow in order to record and plan your time, you should get to know the terminology used in Outlook:

- An *appointment* impacts on your working time but affects only your personal time.
- A *meeting* impacts on your working time but it also affects the time of people participating in the meeting.
- An *event* is an activity spanning a whole day but not affecting your own time. A yearly event is periodical.

Customise your working week on the basis of your various activities. For example, if you do not work on Wednesdays, or you play golf every Friday afternoon. Obviously, you are well aware of these portions of free time and do not need reminding of them, but if one of your colleagues wants to arrange a meeting, he or she might not know that you are not available on Fridays after 4 pm.

To customise your working week:

1. Click on **Tools**, **Options**.

2. Click on the **Calendar Options** button. Define your choices – work day, first day of week, start and end time (Figure 10.1).

Figure 10.1 Customising your working week with the Calendar Options dialog box.

Views

Outlook allows you to modify the Calendar view: click on **View, Current View**. In the sub-menu, select a view.

By default, a single day is displayed in Calendar. If you wish to modify this setting, click on one of the buttons in the toolbar – Day, Work Week, and so on (Figure 10.2).

Figure 10.2 The main types of view

Recording an appointment

To record an appointment, you have a choice of two procedures: one is quick and simple, the other is slightly longer but more accurate.

To create an appointment quickly, click on the date you want on the dates panel. The selected date is displayed in the work time. Click on the required time box. Type a brief description of your appointments, then press **Enter** to confirm.

To create a more detailed appointment, click on the **New** button in the Standard toolbar. The Untitled – Appointment dialog box is displayed (Figure 10.3). If necessary, click on the **Appointment** tab. Specify the following options:

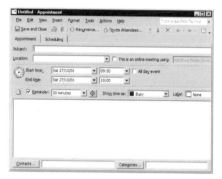

Figure 10.3 The Appointment dialog box.

- **Subject**. Allows you to enter a description of the appointment.
- **Location**. Allows you to specify the appointment address.
- **Start time**. Opens a drop-down list of dates and times. If the appointment is likely to last for the whole day, tick the **All day event** check box.
- **End time**. Opens a drop-down list that allows you to specify the estimated end date and time for the appointments.
- **Reminder**. Allows you to activate or deactivate a sound signal and to specify how long before the appointment you wish to be reminded.
- **Attendee Availability**. Allows you to specify the status of a time block. For example, when you are on a training course, you will mark such a day with the 'Out of Office' option.

■ **Text box**. Allows you to enter additional information concerning the appointment.

Once you have finished specifying options, click on the **Save and Close** button. Your appointment will be displayed in your work time window (Figure 10.4). According to the options you have chosen, a number of symbols are displayed to allow you to see the appointments options at a glance.

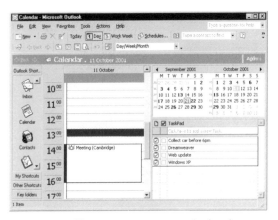

Figure 10.4 The new appointment is displayed.

To move an appointment within the same day, click on its time box with the mouse button pressed, then drag into the new time box.

To delete an appointment, click with the right mouse button on the appointment time box, then select **Clear**.

To change the length of an appointment, drag the upper or lower border of the appointment time box.

Regular appointments

If an appointment occurs on a regular basis, you can enter the appointment once only, specifying that it is regular.

To create a regular appointment:

1. Double-click on the regular appointment time box or click on the **New** button. Click on the **Recurrence** button in the dialog box toolbar (Figure 10.5).

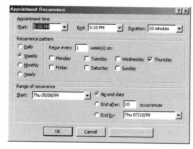

Figure 10.5 The Appointment Recurrence dialog box.

2. Specify the recurrence pattern, duration, range of recurrence, and so on. Click on **OK** to confirm your choice in the Recurrence dialog box. Click on the **Save and Close** button in the **Appointment** dialog box.

Planning a meeting

When you are planning your next business meeting, you no longer need to make all those telephone calls to find out which days people are available. Outlook puts the Appointment Manager at your disposal, allowing you to specify the time range that is likely to suit everybody. Note that this can work only if all your colleagues also use Outlook, and their work time schedules are correct and up to date.

To organise a meeting:

1. Click on **New, New Appointment**. Provide all the specifications for the meeting (date, time, and so on). Click on the **Attendee Availability** tab, then on the **Invite others** button. The **Select Attendees and Resources** dialog box is displayed: this lists the various contacts created in the address book (Figure 10.6).

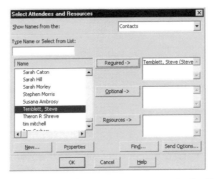

Figure 10.6 Selecting participants in the Select Attendees and Resources dialog box.

2. If required, click on the arrow of the **Name** drop-down list, then click on the address book you wish to use to choose the names of the participants: **Contacts, Outlook Address book** or **Personal Address book**. To invite somebody to the meeting, click on their name in the list, then on one of the buttons on the right (**Required, Optional** and **Resources**). Click on **OK** when all the participants have been included.

3. To check the availability of each participant, click on their name, then use the scroll bar in the planning area to select a time when everybody is available (Figure 10.7). Alternatively, click on the **AutoPick** button to show the next available time block suitable to all participants. When you have found a time that suits everybody, drag the vertical bars that mark the start and the end of the meeting. Click with the right mouse button on the icon in front of each participant and select **Send meeting to this attendee**. Click on **Send** and close the dialog box.

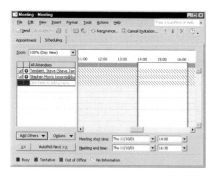

Figure 10.7 Verifying the availability of participants at your meeting.

Outlook sends the invitation to all listed people. Their replies will arrive in your Inbox folder.

Recording an event

Events allows you to remember important dates.

To record an event, click on **Actions, New All Day event** (Figure 10.8). Specify the event subject. Type the event place in the **Location** option. Click on the arrow of the **Start time** option, then select a date. Click on the arrow of the **End time** option, then select the date. If necessary, tick the **All day event** option. If you want to, tick the **Reminder** check box, then click on the arrow and select how long before the event you wish Outlook to send out the sound signal. You can also specify your availability, put down some comments, and select a category. Once you have finished, click on the **Save and Close** button.

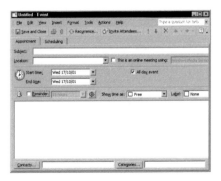

Figure 10.8 Creating an event is quick and easy.

The event is displayed, greyed out, in the work time of the relevant day.

To delete an event, click on it in the work time, then click on the **Clear** button in the Standard toolbar.

Sending and receiving e-mail messages

When you start Outlook for the first time, the Inbox contains a welcome message from Microsoft. Afterwards, all messages will be displayed in this folder. The Inbox folder is displayed by default when you start Outlook.

To have better control of your messages, check the markers displayed as column headers at the top of the receive area (Figure 10.9):

- **Importance**. The presence of this icon indicates that the sender has given the message priority.

- **Icon**. Shows a sealed envelope. When you double-click on a message to read it, the envelope opens.

- **Flag status**. Displays a flag if you have chosen to mark the message to read it again later or to reply to it.

- **Attachment**. Specifies that the sender has attached a file to the message. You can either view the attached file, or you can save it on disk.

- **From**. Displays the sender's name.

- **Subject**. Displays a brief description of the contents of the message.

- **Received**. Displays the date and time the message was received.

To read a message, double-click on it in the list.

*To modify an event, double-click on the event in the work time. Carry out your modifications in the dialog box, then click on the **Save and Close** button.*

Figure 10.9 The Inbox displays all the e-mail messages you have received.

To sort messages according to their subject or their importance, click on the header corresponding to the marker you wish to use to sort your messages. For example, if you wish to sort your messages by importance, click on **Importance**.

If you wish the markers to be displayed in a different order, click on the header to be moved, then drag it to where you want it to be. To delete one of the headers, click on it, then drag it outside the bar.

The **My Shortcuts** button at the bottom of the Outlook bar offers other e-mail folders. This group allows you to sort sent messages, messages to be sent later, and deleted items.

E-mail configuration

For Outlook to display your mail, you must tell it which e-mail service you are working with.

Once you have installed the directory service program, add it to the list of services that Outlook can use:

1. Click on **Tools, Accounts**: the directory services that Outlook can currently use are listed.
2. Click on the **Add** button, then on the name of the service in the list, and then on **OK**.

3. The wizard may ask for additional information depending on the directory service you wish to install. For example, it may ask for your name and fax number, or to select the fax/modem you are going to use. When you have finished, click on **OK**.

Now, you can use Outlook to manage your messages.

Sending messages

To create a message, click on the **New** button in the Standard toolbar (Figure 10.10). In the **To** text box, type the e-mail address of the person to whom you are sending the message. If you have this stored in the Contacts folder, you do not need to type it all over again. Simply click on the **To** button, then select the name of the person from the list in the dialog box. If you wish to send a copy of this message to another person, click on the **Cc** button, then select the person to whom you wish to send the copy from the list or type their e-mail address in the text box. When you want to enter several addresses, separate them with a semi-colon (;).

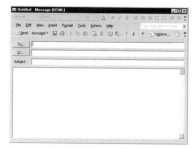

Figure 10.10 Creating an e-mail message.

Once you have filled the addressee boxes, fill in the **Subject** box. Then, in the bottom part of the window, type your message. If you are sending only text, click on the **Send** button. If you wish to attach a file to your message or indicate an option in terms of importance, choose one of the following procedures:

- To format the text, drag your pointer on to the relevant text, then choose font, size and attributes in the toolbar.
- To attach a file to your message, click on the **Insert File** button, then select the file you wish to attach.
- To flag the message, click on the **Flag for Follow Up** button. In the dialog box, specify the options (**Flag to, Clear Flag, Due by,** and so on).
- To indicate the degree of importance for the message, click on the **Importance: High** or **Importance: Low** buttons.

Figure 10.11 E-mail message options.

- The **Options** button offers other choices to create buttons for tracking, accepting and refusing messages (Figure 10.11).

Receiving messages

When you are working in Outlook and you want to know whether you have received any new messages, click on **Tools, Check New Mail** or press **F5**. Outlook then connects to the installed server, retrieves your messages, and displays them in your Inbox.

To read your message, double-click on it. Outlook displays the message in the window. This window offers various buttons:

- **Reply**. Allows you to send a reply message to the sender. Click on this button to open a message window with the sender's address (the person who has sent you the original message to which you are now replying). The text of the original message is also displayed in the text box. You can clear it or keep it. Type your reply, then click on the **Send** button.

- **Reply All**. Allows you to send a reply to all the people on the **To** or **Cc** lists.

- **Transfer**. Allows you to send the message directly to another person.

- **Back** or **Next**. Allows you to scroll through all your messages.

Index